Revised and Updated Edition

Stock Market Profits
and
Higher Income
For You

BY

David R. Sargent

PRESIDENT, UNITED BUSINESS SERVICE
BOSTON, MASSACHUSETTS

SIMON AND SCHUSTER
New York

Designed by Irving Perkins
Manufactured in the United States of America

2   3   4   5   6   7   8   9   10   11

Library of Congress Cataloging in Publication Data

Sargent, David R.
  Stock market profits and higher income for you.
  1. Investments. I.   Title.
HG4521.S3343   1975   332.6'78   74-16023
            ISBN 0-671-21923-5

Portions of this book have previously appeared in
the *United Business and Investment Report* in a different form

Contents

Foreword

Rampant inflation, soaring interest rates, political disequilibrium (meaning Watergate and its aftermath) during much of the early 1970s conspired to depress the stock market regularly to almost unheard-of depths. At least, prices repeatedly fell lower in relation to fundamental values than they had in the investing lifetime of any of us in middle age.

So vengeful was the decline at times that many an investor simply said, "Never again. Give me my savings bank and you can have the stock market."

Naturally, it is at just such times as these that the foundations of tomorrow's fortunes are laid. As every insomniac knows, it's always darkest just before the dawn, both in the bedroom and in the soul.

For those of us who had spent a lifetime, or nearly one, in the investment business, the stock market troubles of these years seemed as likely to be transitory as had all the others of the past half century. After all, even the Great Depression of the 1930s finally ended, only to be followed by one of the longest bull markets in history.

As the old Cape Codder responded to the anxious tourist's query about whether the rain would ever stop, "It always has, ma'am."

7

This book is written to help the individual investor do something with his savings that will give him reasonable security and a fighting chance to beat the rampant inflation of our times. Procedures and approaches discussed here could even produce handsome profits from time to time.

I don't expect readers of this treatise to be Wall Street experts, but I do expect them to be sophisticated enough to know that you can't get something for nothing in the stock and bond markets any more than you can in the real world.

As psychotherapist Sheldon B. Kopp has said, "The victims of confidence men are always those secret thieves who hope to get something for nothing. That great psychologist, W. C. Fields, used to say: 'You can't cheat an honest man.' " There's no question about it, if you expect something for nothing, stay out of the stock market.

Thus, readers of this book should be looking for practical help in building a decent savings program. They should greet all fervid blandishments from the world of finance with a discreet yawn. They should know by instinct that there are no more wizards on Wall Street than on Main Street.

Successful investment requires psychological maturity, therefore, on the part of the investor as well as accurate information on the securities in question. Perhaps maturity is even more important than information. Certainly one can make more progress by simply buying the shares of the nation's leading corporations and sitting with them long term, through peace and war, boom and recession, than one is likely to make jumping feverishly in and out of the stocks that have been exhaustively researched.

This book reflects the gleanings of a generation (*Webster's*— "generation: the average span of time between the birth of parents and that of their offspring") of experience in the world of stocks and bonds on the part of the author, plus distillations of the knowledge and experience of a large professional staff here at United Business Service. Outstanding among the members of the staff who worked on this project has been our Business Editor, Ronald K. Devine, who made major contributions to the writing, organization, and editing. Ron, all of our other editors, CFA's, investment counselors, commodity experts, and many others, male and female, old and young, have kept their keen minds endlessly at work in an attempt to find a way to happy savings and eventual prosperity for the average investor.

We think this book does it, and invite you to try for yourself and see.

DAVID R. SARGENT

January 1976

The Back Yard

On the back page of each week's *United Business and Investment Report* there has appeared for decades a column entitled "The Back Yard." New readers are often somewhat taken aback and wonder what the little editorials are all about.

"After all," they say, "I buy your weekly Bulletins for up-to-date business and financial information plus specific investment advice. What are your 'Back Yard' editorials, usually not even on business or investment subjects, supposed to mean to me?"

Our answer to our readers is that the pieces are written to help them get to know us, to show them what we are really like, what we think about life in general. Just as neighbors chatting over the back fence on a variety of subjects get to know one another pretty well, reading these mini-editorials will give our readers a glimpse of the real "us."

We tell them they should get the idea that since we are just people, we are not likely to be infallible. We have specialized education and training, and experience measured in decades, but we will not be right every time.

These Back Yards, being usually in a lighter vein, offer some counterpoint to the heavier prose on the inside pages. I hope you like them.

D. R. S.

Defining and Fulfilling Your Investment Aims

THE BACK YARD

Many an investor wonders these days whether common stocks really are an effective inflation hedge after all. Certainly, if one looks primarily at the Dow a negative conclusion is understandable.

However, if you look at the corporate earning power underlying common stocks, they look better. The steady rise in earnings during these years makes stocks more valuable than they used to be, at the same price, and, more important, supports more liberal dividends.

Dividend increases last year, for example, totaled 2,181, nearly three times the 1970 figure and well above the 1,582 boosts reported at the 1968 bull market top. And thanks to some relaxation of the limits on distribution by the Committee on Interest and Dividends, payments have been generously larger in recent weeks.

According to the Commerce Department figures for all corporations, the record looks like this:

	Profits	Dividends
1973	+27%	+7%
1972	+16	+4
1971	+21	+2
1970	−12	+2
1969	− 6	+3

Earnings have gained so fast in recent years that the dividend payout on average is only 40%, against the more traditional 50%. Today's payout is the lowest in 18 years. That being the case, another generous increase in dividends seems a fair expectation for investors in 1974. Happy thought.

JANUARY 21, 1974

1

What Hope for the Little Fellow?

Several years ago we wrote:

> As the cost of running a brokerage business has risen,
> interest in the modest commissions paid by the small investor
> has fallen. Big customers are preferred for they pay more.
> And as the small investor is frozen out of the marketplace,
> the number of buyers and sellers diminishes.
>
> Meantime, the institutional investor gets bigger and bigger.
> As the market loses the dependable diversity of many minds,
> opinions, and decisions, it becomes even more sensitive to
> the shifts of opinion of the few and the mighty. And with
> more and more fund managers driving for performance, the
> effects can be capricious indeed.*

And we were right. Small investors abandoned the market in
droves, leaving Wall Street in the clutch of mammoth institutional investors who proved as fickle as they were powerful. The
result was as erratic a stock market as has ever been seen and a
growing conviction in the minds of many small investors that
they were right to have left.

* *United Business and Investment Report,* April 27, 1970.

15

Somewhat more recently, Bradford Cook, then chairman of the Securities and Exchange Commission, suggested that the small investor was fast becoming an "endangered species." Of course, the commissioner was thinking of the problem from an industry point of view. By way of evidence, two thirds of the trading on the New York Stock Exchange was estimated as institutional in September 1973. The loss of the individual investor meant a loss of commissions, and by the early 1970s the brokerage fraternity was literally staggering from a precipitous revenue loss in the face of soaring costs. As firm after firm failed or merged with stronger brethren, some in the industry, such as the quoted SEC chairman, began to wonder whether abandoning the little fellow had been altogether wise. He may not have been as profitable for the broker as the institution. However, he did represent volume in the aggregate, and for an industry fast approaching insolvency, any additional income was manna indeed.

Some suggestion of industry enlightenment at last occurred in early 1974 when Merrill Lynch, Pierce, Fenner and Smith, the nation's largest brokerage house and industry pacesetter, cut commissions on small trades in response to the SEC's move to free from fixed fees trades of $2,000 or less. This was a conscious attempt to lure back the small investor. Let's hope it works, for the good of all investors, big and little.

Before that, as closely as could be measured, the individual investor apparently had opted out. The steady yearly increase in the number of shareholders estimated by the New York Stock Exchange tapered off markedly in the early 1972 tally and actually declined in the following two years—from 32.5 million down to 31.7 million, then to 30.9 million. Mutual funds, a haven largely for the small investor, reported an excess of redemptions over sales in 1972, 1973, 1974, and 1975. The industry that had been the belle of the financial ball in the 1960s clearly was the number one wallflower of the 1970s.

WHAT HAPPENED

A glance at the performance of the stock market in recent years will give some indication of the experience many investors had.

SOURCES OF N.Y.S.E. PUBLIC VOLUME-

PERCENTAGE DISTRIBUTION

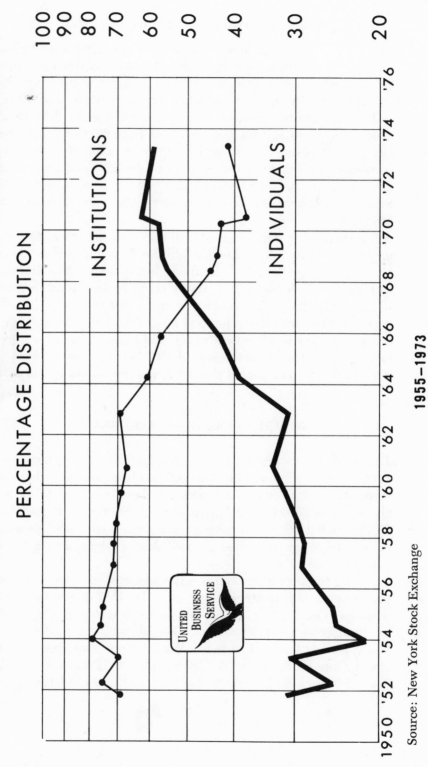

INSTITUTIONS

INDIVIDUALS

UNITED BUSINESS SERVICE

1955–1973

Source: New York Stock Exchange

First, consider the accompanying chart, showing the familiar Dow-Jones Industrial Average. According to this venerable indicator, common stock holders made no progress at all from 1963 on. This was during a period when prices at home rose by 27% and the purchasing power of the dollar declined by 22%. Meantime, interest on savings accounts rose from 5% to 8% and even 10%, U.S. Treasury bond yields rose from 5.25% to 6.5%, good corporate bond yields climbed from 6% to 7.5%, and high grade tax-free municipal bond yields marched up from 4.5% to 5.5%. Small wonder that the tide of investor dollars ebbed from Wall Street.

But even these stark contrasts tell only half the story. As many investors will ruefully acknowledge, the Dow Industrials almost always do better than an individual's list of stocks. As a startling "for instance," consider that the average mutual fund (professionally managed, mind you!) was up by 30% in 1975, while the good old Dow Industrials jumped a full 40%. Many an individual investor could easily bemoan, as one did to us, "You fellows keep talking about the market being off 10%. What I want to know is what market you're talking about, because my stocks are off 50%."

WHICH AVERAGE DO YOU READ?

This leads us to discuss the various measures or indexes that people use to tell where the "market" has been. Because there are more than 1,500 common shares on the New York Stock Exchange, about 800 on the American Stock Exchange, and another 25,000 traded off the regular exchanges, or "over-the-counter," finding an index that gives a good idea of where all stocks are going isn't easy.

Among the poorest measures is the one most old-time investors, professional and amateur alike, use: the Dow-Jones Industrial Average. The Dow is inadequate because it represents such a small sampling—only 30 of the 1,500-odd issues on the New York Stock Exchange. Furthermore, few of these are real growth stocks. Only Eastman Kodak, General Electric, Procter & Gamble, Sears, Roebuck & Co., and perhaps Allied Chemical have turned

DOW PRICES, PROFITS, P/E'S - & GNP

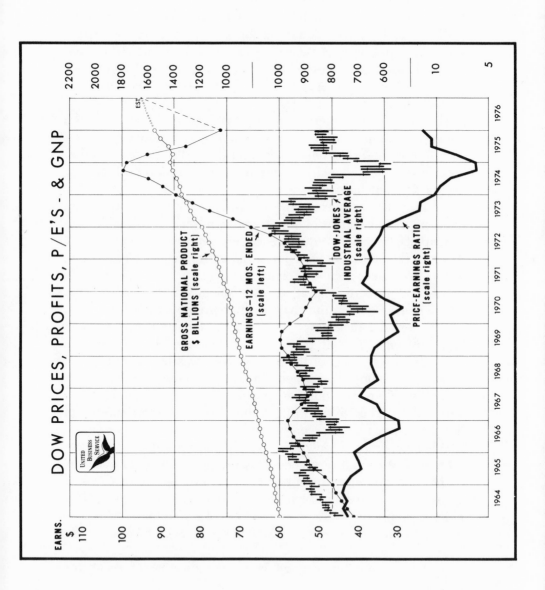

GROSS NATIONAL PRODUCT
$ BILLIONS (scale right)

EARNINGS—12 MOS. ENDED
(scale left)

DOW-JONES
INDUSTRIAL AVERAGE
(scale right)

PRICE-EARNINGS RATIO
(scale right)

UNITED
BUSINESS
SERVICE

EARNS.
$
110
100
90
80
70
60
50
40
30

2200
2000
1800
1600
1400
1200
1000

1000
900
800
700
600

10

5

1964 1965 1966 1967 1968 1969 1970 1971 1972 1973 1974 1975 1976

in above-average performances in recent years. Three of the Dow stocks are oils, representing an industry that has had an ongoing series of troubles, from feisty Arab hosts abroad to equally troublesome (for them) ecologists at home.

The list also includes three big chemical companies, two big steels, two nonferrous metals, two of the big three auto makers, two container companies, and, to top it all off, one big aerospace company and American Telephone. None of these industries (and therefore the companies within them) has enjoyed significant earnings growth for some time, and the hapless Dow has two representatives in almost every one.

The venerable average has next to no representation in the dynamic growth areas of our economy—leisure time, pollution control, health, services generally, and the "pill." These and other areas dominate the market and have a marked effect on the averages that include them.

Because the broader averages have greater representation in the more dynamic areas of our economy, they do better in periods of market strength. They more closely represent what is really going on than does the Dow-Jones Industrial Average. This shows clearly in the accompanying chart.

However, before leaping to the conclusion that one of the broader "averages" in the chart really represents the market, it is well to consider their flaws. The essential fallacy of the so-called broad averages is that they, too, are distorted. The distortion comes from weighting of the price of the stock by the number of shares outstanding. Thus, each share in the Standard & Poor's 500 is multiplied by the number of shares of that particular issue outstanding. This gives IBM roughly 365 times the influence of Acme Markets, for instance.

When this sort of weighting is used, just one good performer such as IBM can offset several hundred poor actors. As evidence of the distortion inherent in the weighted averages, take a look at an unweighted average such as the Value Line Composite. This index is simply the average of the prices of 1,400 stocks. As can be seen, it is far behind the S&P 500, and still some 60% below the 1968 peak.

If the unweighted average is more indicative of what the

WHICH AVERAGE DO YOU READ?

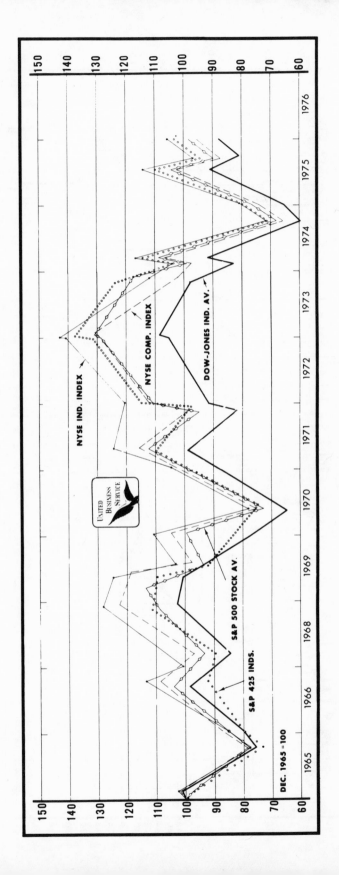

Sources: Dow Jones & Co., New York Stock Exchange, Standard & Poor's

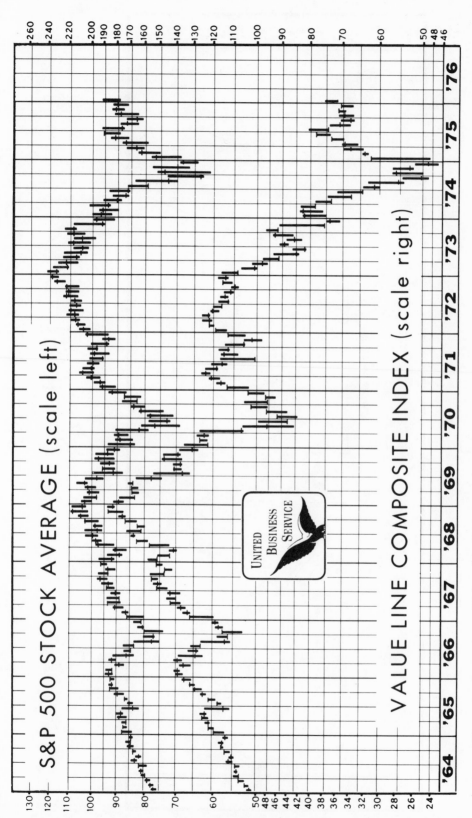

S&P 500 STOCK AVERAGE (scale left)

VALUE LINE COMPOSITE INDEX (scale right)

Used by permission of Arnold Bernhard & Co., Inc., and
Standard & Poor's

"average" stock has been doing in recent years, it is small wonder that the individual still has a preference for the savings bank over the stock market.

BUT THERE IS HOPE—GO FIRST CLASS

Before despairing over stocks and seeking permanent shelter in the savings bank, it is well to note that while the stock market and most indicators thereof have done poorly in recent years, a good many stocks have done very well. Investors who have held such market leaders as American Home Products, Caterpillar Tractor, Eastman Kodak, Procter & Gamble, Standard Oil of Indiana, and Weyerhaeuser (we are intentionally omitting such wonder stocks as Digital Equipment) have done very well indeed.

And one hardly needed to be clairvoyant or possess extra-sensory perception to find stocks such as these back in the 1960s. The trouble is that most investors—and the institutions were worse in this respect than many individual investors—were too carried away by the thought of instant riches to fool around with everyday blue chips. As a man said to us once, "I don't have to pay you to tell me to buy the American Home Products; that everyone knows about. What I want is tomorrow's wonder drug company, not today's aspirin maker."

In those days the crowd ran off after the conglomerates (Litton traced an arc from 20 to 100 to 10 in ten exciting years), the health-care newcomers (Four Seasons Nursing from 5½ to 90¾ and back practically to 0 in five or six years), or the big new youth market (National Student Marketing, from 1½ to 35¾ and then back to 50¢ in 1968–70). Then there was Memorex, which back in the 1960s was one of the white-hot hopes of the burgeoning computer software industry. It went from 8 to 170 to 0 in nine years.

The stocks to buy in those halcyon years were not the *wunderkinder*, but the tried and true. Consider what a portfolio of the aforementioned blue chips would have done for the investor with the wisdom and patience to buy for the long pull, even if he bought them at the market high (about 1000 on the Dow) in 1968. For the sake of illustration, let's suppose our "intelligent" investor had put about $1,000 into each.

Shares Now Held°	Dec. 1968° Price	Amount	Price Dec. 1975	Amount	Gain
48 American Home Products	20	$ 960	37	$ 1,776	85%
20 Caterpillar Tractor	44	880	68	1,380	55
30 Eastman Kodak	37	1,110	107	3,210	189
20 Procter & Gamble	43	860	92	1,840	114
30 Standard Oil (Indiana)	30	900	43	1,290	43
50 Weyerhaeuser	21	1,050	36	1,800	71
		$5,760		$11,296	84%

° Adjusted for stock splits.

This table and those that follow are intended to show trends and relationships. They are based on the most authoritative data available at the time of compilation, but they have been simplified as much as possible to avoid undue clutter. For the sake of uniformity, they have been constructed using December 1975 securities prices as the most recent quotation. Dividend figures are expressed as the indicated 1975 rates. Where possible, earnings figures are actual fiscal 1975. Where these are not available, they are the estimates as of December 1975. Price-earnings ratios are computed by dividing the December 1975 price by the figure in the 1975 earnings column. Yields are computed by dividing the 1975 dividend by the December 1975 price.

Although it is too much to believe that our "intelligent" investor would have picked this half dozen and no other—he could just as easily have picked General Motors or an electric or gas utility—he would not have needed genius to select this group. First, the nation was on a health kick in the late 1960s (and still is). Health had been important in the Kennedy Administration and in the succeeding "Great Society," and public buying of "medicine" of all kinds was in a steady uptrend. Meantime, American Home Products had an enviable record of regular annual growth in sales and earnings, which had just as regularly been translated into increased dividends and, almost as regularly, into higher stock prices. What's more, the company made aspirin—as common a product as you could ask.

Much the same pattern worked for Caterpillar Tractor. With highly visible products rolling out a road system of well-known prime national priority, Caterpillar, too, had an excellent record.

Eastman Kodak, meeting a steady rise in demand from an ever more affluent public, was no unknown. Procter & Gamble, the biggest maker of soap, cleanliness, and godliness the world had ever seen, was a household name with an enviable record.

Standard Oil of Indiana was a big well-known integrated oil company of a largely domestic nature. This meant it would have no trouble from such "native" uprisings as have been seen regularly in the Middle East while it continued to prosper nicely from the steady uptrend in oil consumption. Weyerhaeuser was another household name—at least in households that had anything to do with building houses, their own or other people's. The company's record was excellent, and with housing apparently in chronic short supply, future performance was likely to be as good.

And so they went, the big names in industry that had great records and no demonstrable problems in the discernible future. They didn't have the steady pressure of foreign competition that threatened the steel and auto industries. They didn't have the recurring regulatory problems of the electric and gas people. Neither were they in fiercely competitive areas where industrial throatcutting was a matter of common experience—such as in semiconductors, aluminum, and paper.

PLAN TO GET RICH SLOWLY

The same sort of investment opportunities are around today. Thus, there is every reason to believe that the individual investor can put his savings in the stock market and watch them grow. He (or she) can buy stocks without fear of being trampled by the clumsy institutional investor. All he needs are a few simple rules, an idea of where to look, and the understanding that the only safe and sure way to get rich is slowly.

2

Rules to Invest By

Rule number one is to determine first what you want your savings to do for you—before you buy anything. Are you putting your savings aside for a rainy day, some indeterminate day in the future, or are you setting some dollars aside to meet the costs of a college education that is coming along right on schedule? Perhaps you want to build a retirement fund which won't really be needed for years—or maybe your savings will have to produce income now, immediate "eating money."

These questions are important, for they will determine whether you should invest for capital growth or current income. Most of the time you will have to accept one or the other. Rare indeed is the investment that offers a goodly share of both. The answers to such questions will tell you also how much risk you can reasonably assume. The person needing "eating money" now can tolerate much less risk than the investor building for a far-off retirement.

Let's illustrate these choices with a few "for instances." Consider the midcareer salaried individual who can divert regular amounts of income from his family's spending stream to savings. His aim is a retirement fund to supplement his company pension.

As is the case with most of us who labor in the corporate vineyard, the Internal Revenue Service enjoys a generous share of his income. Since his earned income is already more than he needs for regular expenses and his investment aim is essentially long term, there is no point in shooting for investment income now and further sharing with Uncle Sam. What this man wants is capital growth and low or no investment income.

Further, since his salary is already more than he "needs," he can assume a bit of extra risk. In other words, he takes a modestly larger chance in the hope of better-than-average gains, for if he loses he can, theoretically anyway, replace the lost dollars from regular earned income. The portfolio, or list of stocks, of a person in this financial position should look something like this, at least at the start:

No. of Shares	Quality Rating*	Dec. 1975 Price	1975 Earnings	Earnings Gain Per Year 1971– 1974	P/E Ratio	Amount	Yield
75 American Express	H	39	$2.50	17%	16	$ 2,925	2.0%
75 American Home Products	H	37	1.55	16	24	2,775	2.4
70 Citicorp	H	29	3.00	22	10	2,030	3.0
200 Damon Corp.	S	9	.27	19	33	1,800	2.2
75 Georgia-Pacific	M	44	2.50	56	18	3,300	1.8
100 Peabody-Galion	S	15	1.60	27	9	1,500	0.5
85 Perkin-Elmer	M	25	1.08	14	23	2,125	1.2
70 Pfizer	H	28	2.15	14	13	1,960	2.7
75 Southwestern Life	H	26	2.55	15	10	1,950	2.1
60 Utah International	M	46	4.20	52	11	2,760	2.2
						$23,125	2.0%

* H–high; M–medium; S–speculative.

SOME SAFE, SOME CHANCY

Note that five of the ten stocks suggested are rated top quality, whereas three are medium and two are speculative. Theoretically, then, the two essentially speculative issues involve the most risk and amount to a relatively small percentage of the total investment. Meantime, fully half of the funds are in top-quality issues and involve a minimum chance of loss.

Now, you may ask, what makes Damon and Peabody-Galion speculative and the others high-grade? Well, the five high-grade issues represent big seasoned concerns with excellent long-term records. Relatively speaking, Damon and Peabody-Galion are newcomers. Damon's growth is predicated on the company's ability to continue expanding its chain of pathological labs. It has a new diagnostic test for cancer awaiting clearance by the authorities. Will it be cleared, and if it is, will the medical profession use it in volume? Or will this new test be replaced by a better one, put out by someone else?

Peabody-Galion is big in pollution control, but so are others. Whose products and processes will win out over the long term? Much pollution-control effort reflects federal funds and the Administration's sense of urgency. How much of either will the industry enjoy—one, two, or more years from now? Dividends were initiated on the common shares in the summer of 1972. By way of comparison, dividends have been paid by American Home Products since 1919.

And so it goes. The conservative stocks have broad dependable product lines with reasonably assured future demand. The speculative situations are much newer and more specialized. In the foregoing portfolio, Georgia-Pacific, Perkin-Elmer, and Utah International fall somewhere in between.

FEET FIRST AND BIT BY BIT

Most people save bit by bit and cannot start an investment program all at once, with a big splash. Even if they could, they shouldn't. As with most things in life, investing should be done carefully and slowly. For example, to go in all at once might mean buying everything at a temporary market peak. While this would likely matter little on a long-term basis, it could be very discomfiting short term, particularly for the beginner. So the best thing is to start slowly, buying one at a time over a period of weeks, always buying the high-grade stocks first and the speculations last.

Finally, let us suggest that the man who earns more than he needs should be very nearly 100% in common stocks. All he needs in the savings bank is a fund for emergencies. Such a fund would vary in size with the life-style of the family and the number and ages of those therein. Naturally, if a family has older children approaching college age, the savings bank account should begin to reflect the realities of today's (or better yet, tomorrow's!) tuition and other college costs. On the other hand, if the kids are little or—happy circumstance—have completed the educational process, much less is needed in a cash reserve fund. Similarly, the family with limited health insurance coverage needs more in the savings account than one with the usual cradle-to-grave coverage offered by most major corporations today.

INVESTING FOR INCOME NOW

Now, as another specific investment situation, let's consider the plight of the working girl of "middle years" whose pay just barely covers her "needs." Let's suppose she inherits or otherwise comes by $25,000, a sum of money that not only is large in relation to anything she has ever had before, but is a piece of good fortune that is not likely to be repeated. In other words, "This is it." What does she do?

Well, she opts for income now, with plenty of safety. She buys the shares of companies that have excellent dividend records and every likelihood of being able to pay as regularly and liberally in the future as they have in the past. There are companies that fit this description. Because they also often have very slim long-term growth prospects, their shares usually offer a comparatively high return. Consider this example:

No. of Shares	Dec. 1975 Price	Amount	1975 Dividend	Dividend Paid Since	Yield
200 American Electric Power	21	$ 4,200	$2.00	1910	9.5%
100 American Telephone	50	5,000	3.40	1881	6.8
100 Chase Manhattan	28	2,800	2.20	1848	7.9
200 Gulf Oil	21	4,200	1.70	1936	8.1
100 Hackensack Water	27	2,700	2.48	1887	9.2
100 Pennwalt	28	2,800	1.36	1863	4.9
100 U.S. Fidelity & Guaranty	36	3,600	2.48	1939	6.9
	Total = $25,300			Average Yield = 7.6%	

Note the average yield here, 7.6%, compared with the meager 2.0% available in the growth portfolio discussed a few pages back. The yield here is high because the growth potential is low. By growth we mean earnings-per-share growth, not growth in gross sales or revenues. Each of the preceding companies is enjoying revenue or sales growth, but not real earnings growth. Each has a problem. American Electric Power and American Telephone & Telegraph face a chronic earnings squeeze between the rising costs of an inflationary period and lagging rate relief as regulatory bodies express their reluctance to hit the already over-burdened consumer (and voter!) with even higher prices.

Gulf's problem is easy to see—the Arabs. Hackensack Water has a problem much like that of American Electric Power and AT&T. In addition, it is not easy to increase the supply of water it has for sale. Chase Manhattan is suffering from investors' fears for the fate of New York itself. If the "Big Apple" goes under, will Chase Manhattan go too? Our answer is no.

Pennwalt's problem is more psychological than real—the market today simply does not rate heavy-industry stocks very high. Hence, the generous yield. Since this sentiment could easily change, Pennwalt might sell substantially higher someday. U.S. Fidelity & Guaranty is another one that could sell much higher someday. It is down now because underwriting earnings (the profit it makes on its insurance business) are down, leaving investment income to carry the day—which it does, and nicely. Thus, dividends are safe here, thanks to the company's investment income, and when underwriting profits turn around the stock should bounce back.

YOU CAN HAVE SOME OF BOTH

This safe and sane program gives our "middle years" investor good income, few worries, and some modest chance of seeing her money grow over the long term. The difference between this income program and the growth plan suggested for the man with "extra" money is rather extreme. Lots of people fall somewhere in between and would like a little of both—income today and some

capital growth for tomorrow. This can be done easily, as long as
the investor accepts the obvious trade-offs. Generally speaking,
the more growth potential you get, the lower is the income that
comes with it, and vice versa.

LONG SHOTS, SHORT SHOTS, AND HOT SHOTS

Before closing this chapter we should pay some attention to those
who like to take chances, particularly if there is a possibility of
financial gain. Some people just don't like to be safe and sane.
They ride motorcycles, hunt with bow and arrow, and when
things get too sticky at home they go sky diving.

This type of person wants some fun out of his investments. The
protective coloration of this sort of character is diverse and invariably misleading. It could lurk behind the rimless glasses and
diffident smile of the telephone company bookkeeper or in the
heart of his matronly working wife.

QUICKIES ARE HARD TO FIND

A married couple of this nature would be earning more than they
need. Home mortgage would be long since paid off and car
payments a thing of their youthful past. Childless, secure, and
eminently staid, this couple would love to, believe it or not, make
a fast buck in the stock market.

What a couple such as this should do is run counter to the
trend. For example, when the oil shortage hit in November of
1973, any stock related to travel literally disintegrated. Sober
American Express fell 42% in a matter of weeks, from 64 to 37.
More volatile AMF dropped 48%. By midwinter 1973/1974 it
became obvious that the Arabs would sooner or later lift the
embargo, that they had not fallen into the arms of Mother Russia,
that travel by auto was not forever dead. Our thrill-seeking
bookkeeper and wife could have bought these stocks at that
point.

	Pre-Embargo Price*	Embargo Low†	Decline
American Express	62	37	40%
AMF Inc.	33	17	48
Bandag, Inc.	36	22	39
Coleman Co.	15	5	67
Delta Air Lines	54	33	39
Denny's Inc.	17	7	59
Disney (Walt) Prods.	78	35	55
Eastman Kodak	128	96	25
Federated Dept. Stores	42	27	36
Holiday Inns	25	11	56
Howard Johnson	21	9	57
Marriott Corp.	29	15	48
McDonald's Corp.	69	44	36
Monroe Auto Equip.	27	10	63
Northwest Airlines	26	17	35
Ramada Inns	11	4	64
Sears Roebuck	100	78	22
Skyline Corp.	17	9	47
Transcon Lines	12	6	50
UAL, Inc.	24	15	38

* Price on October 5, 1973.
† Lowest price between October 5, 1973, and March 29, 1974.

The point here is to speculate by betting that the market is wrong. When a stock or stock group falls apart, investigate. Why so? Has the change reflected by the market really occurred? Is it permanent? Has the market overdone it again? If so, the smart speculator might well step in.

A LONG LOOK AHEAD

Or suppose we have a young fellow who not only has some extra "bread" but also dreams of buying tomorrow's General Electric today. He would love to stumble upon the second coming of Iréneé duPont hand grinding a bit of gunpowder on the Brandywine. So he looks way ahead.

Is there a way to get oil out of shale? Who is likely to develop it? Can wastes be recycled at a profit? Who can make a dollar out of cleaning our air or water? The big risk in these things is that the problem may be solved in another way or by another technique, or just go away. Technological change is furiously rapid and tough to divine in advance. So money put on the nose of new companies with new products and processes for new areas is money that is often lost.

Sometimes, of course, that kind of money comes home in millions, so for those who can stand the heat, the game is worth the candle. Here are some specifics for the young man with a faraway look in his eyes.

Stock (1975 Dividend)	Dec. 1975 Price	Yield	Comments
Baker Industries ($0.24)	10	2.4%	Has diversified stake in protection services field; 1976 earnings should rise.
Browning-Ferris Inds. ($0.20)	6	3.3	The leader in solid-waste management. Profits should move ahead sharply.
DEKALB ($0.20)	38	0.5	One of the best long-term bets in agribusiness. Leader in hybrid wheat and swine.
Fort Howard Paper ($0.56)	32	1.8	Leading wastepaper recycler with fine record.
Louisiana-Pacific ($0.20)	12	1.7	Applying modern management techniques to lumber production, housing recovery beneficiary.
SEDCO ($0.13)	22	0.6	Probably the leading offshore driller; also has stake in pipeline construction.
Wang Laboratories ($0.10)	10	1.0	Product costs easing and orders picking up from recession low. WCS computer line a big winner.
Waste Management (nil)	7	Nil	Prominent in solid-waste management and headed for impressive sales-earnings growth.

Here again the point is to outsmart everyone else, only it's done by looking further into the future, rather than simply betting that the crowd has overdone it. The chances are large, but so are the possible rewards. For the hot-shot stock buyer, this approach has appeal.

3

On Using Your Head

Rule number two is implicit in the comments made in the first two chapters—buy the best-known companies. Don't try to "beat the market" by unearthing the General Motors of tomorrow. The chances of success are so small even for the professional money manager, not to mention the amateur or part-time investor, as to make a hole in one for the beginning golfer a better bet. So, as a general rule, put your dollars in the tried and true stocks, leaving the financial wildcatting to someone else.

This does not mean that the average investor should resign himself to a financial life with Mother Bell. On the contrary, there are plenty of exciting and promising stocks that come under the heading "tried and true." IBM and Xerox, the wonder stocks of the post–World War II years, fall into this category. So also do a number of promising lesser lights such as Howard Johnson Co., Mesa Petroleum, and Schlitz Brewing. These stocks are no blue chips. They are unquestionably speculative, and they can sink sickeningly in weak markets. However, they have been in business a long time, their products are well known with excellent and dependable markets, and they are financially sound.

Further, their stock prices are reasonable in relation to such earthy fundamentals as assets, earnings, and dividends. In short, there are plenty of attractive, reasonable speculations that offer the promise of real and substantial profit some day for the man or woman who can take the risk. You don't have to go off the reservation to have a good time with your common stocks.

TAKE YOUR TIME

Rule number three is patience. Things rarely work out overnight on Wall Street, and when they do almost everyone is taken by surprise. So, when you buy a good stock, buy it for the long pull. Consider yourself a part owner of the business. You have become one because you believe the business is fundamentally sound and the prospects excellent. Therefore, you don't have to watch the daily gyrations in stock price, with fear in your throat when it is down and exaltation in your soul when it is up.

BURROUGHS WAS ONCE A DOG

As an example, think of the investors who bought Burroughs in the late 1950s and early 1960s because the company was moving into the computer field. The stock had long been a so-so performer, reflecting quite accurately the humdrum existence of an adding machine maker, which is what Burroughs was.

Interest in the shares picked up when the management began to move the company from mechanical machines (remember the hand-crank adding machines?) to electrically operated equipment and then to electronic machines for the accounting trade. Burroughs then headed for computers for banks and other financial institutions.

This meant, of course, flying right in the face of supergiant IBM. Thus, buying Burroughs on speculation that it would move successfully into competition with the industry leader entailed considerable risk. At any rate, buyers of the stock in those years needed patience. The shares sold in the teens for most of the early 1960s except for one brief flurry up into the 20s that ended abruptly in the 1962 market. By 1964 the stock was down to 11, five years after the transformation of the company had begun.

No one could have been faulted for selling out that year. Although the promise of computer excitement was still there, the company had as yet failed to make much money on it, and without earnings—the *sine qua non* of stock prices—there was no market performance. But then in late 1964 earnings turned up and in January 1965 the stock jumped from 12½ to 16. A year later it had nearly doubled, and in five years the stock had gained tenfold. Now, of course, the shares are sailing along close to 90 after still one more 2-for-1 split, for a total gain of 1,500% in a dozen years.

But the key here was patience. Those who waited prospered mightily. Those who wanted their rewards "today" lost out. And in the stock market the impatient usually do. So, if your reasons for liking a particular stock are sound, give the market plenty of time to come around to your point of view.

One way to develop patience with your investments is to think of your commitment in a stock as you do your home, or even your vacation home. You bought your house to fill a specific need after applying certain qualifying tests to it, including price, and it is now presumably serving satisfactorily. As long as your living requirements remain the same and nothing seriously wrong develops with the structure or the neighborhood, you stay with it.

You don't keep checking daily or weekly with your real estate broker to see how its value is changing in relation to other houses around town. And even if you read in the real estate section of the Sunday paper that "home values slump as mortgage money tightens," you don't rush to sell. You realize that any such slippage in price is temporary. With your home, then, you automatically think long term. Do the same with your stocks.

SHORT TERM WON'T WORK

As a perfect example of how *not* to invest, consider this suggestion we got from a local high school principal. He had moved to Boston from another system and carried about $10,000 from his former pension plan to the local one. According to the rules of the game, he didn't have to deposit the $10,000 in the Massachusetts plan right away; he had apparently several months to decide whether to throw in his lot with Massachusetts teachers or do something else with his share of his original pension program.

As many financially inexperienced people are, our principal was entranced with the possibility of seeing his money multiply on Wall Street, while at the same time he wanted the certainty of a real pension at the end of his working years. So he suggested a little of both. He asked us if we would encourage him to put his $10,000 into Standard Oil of California for the two months before the deadline for the usual pension plan. The stock looked very cheap to him, as it really was, historically, and with the gathering fuel crisis, he thought the outlook for the company was great. "What do you think," he asked, "should I do it?"

"Not on your life," was our response. Two months was much too short a time to make a round-trip investment in a common stock, any common stock. No matter how good a value a particular issue might be—and we shared his enthusiasm for Standard Oil of California—there was nothing that would save its price from any temporary market spill that developed.

For example, let's suppose that at just about the time our principal's $10,000 was due to be transferred from Standard Oil of California to the pension fund, the Justice Department announced an intent to explore the possible break-up of the big oil companies into smaller competing parts. Even though this might only be a trial balloon, the oil stocks could well drop 10% in value. The $10,000 would only be $9,000. Part of the pension would be lost irretrievably because one man's circumstances wouldn't let him wait a short while for the stock to come back.

Because there are all kinds of things that can knock the market off temporarily, most of them absolutely unforeseeable, one should never buy a stock with money that will be needed for other purposes within a relatively short time. Invest only for the long pull and only with savings dollars that you don't think you'll need for a long time.

4

Avoid Crowds

Rule number four is an obvious one and makes great sense, but is probably the one most frequently violated by investors, individual and institutional alike. It is—*avoid fads*. If everyone seems to be rushing to buy stocks in a particular industry group, let them. But don't do it yourself. If one seems to be the darling of the day, don't compete. Let the others have it.

Always, as the kids say, "do your own thing." Fads come and go on Wall Street with all the regularity that they do on Madison Avenue or Seventh Avenue. Consider some of the enthusiasms that have swept Wall Street since World War II. Most recent and disastrous was the rush to conglomerates of the 1960s. The best and most amusing description of the inner workings of a conglomerate appeared in Charles Ellis's book, *The Second Crash*.

FINANCIAL LEGERDEMAIN

Put briefly, it worked this way: A growth company with shares selling at a high price-earnings ratio would use its stock to buy the shares of some other company whose shares were selling at a price low in relation to earnings. Once the earnings of the merged company were part of the earnings of the conglomerate, they would be valued at the high P/E of the latter. This again would greatly boost the value of the conglomerate shares.

There were other tricks, too, such as buying a cash-rich company with stock and then trickling the cash out slowly to boost the merging company's—the conglomerate's—earnings regularly each quarter. This would give the stock market the heady picture of ever-rising earnings and push the conglomerate shares even higher. International Telephone and Telegraph was great at this. See Anthony Sampson's *The Sovereign State of ITT*.

FIGURES DON'T LIE

But one didn't have to expose these tricks to see two or three things that would have kept the intelligent investor out of the conglomerate soup at the time. First, it was the very size of the crowd clamoring to buy the shares. There was a place for Litton, LTV Corp., Gulf & Western, and, of course, ITT in nearly every mutual fund, pension, and profit-sharing portfolio. Any experienced investor should know that in this diverse and complex world, nothing is that good!

Second, it was easy to see that no real economic gain was coming from the merging of unlike companies in unrelated businesses into giant conglomerates. In other words, if the economy wasn't gaining from the construction of these giants, if the whole was not making any more of a contribution to the economy than the sum of the parts, why were their shares so much more attractive than those of ordinary line companies?

Third, size usually works against efficiency. There hasn't been a President in the past twenty-five years who hasn't called the federal bureaucracy "sprawling," "inert," or "unmanageable." Think of what has been said about the manageability of the Department of Health, Education, and Welfare alone in recent years. If big and diverse government is hard to manage, why isn't the same true for private enterprise when it gets just as big and diverse?

ONE-EYED MUTUAL FUNDS

Some of the fads right after World War II spawned mutual funds specialized in covering just one industry. If there was ever a contradiction in terms, these narrowly concentrated funds were it. The very *raison d'être* of the mutual fund is to give the small investor diversification, something that is very difficult to do on his own, if indeed it is possible at all. Thus, to concentrate his dollars in one industry made little sense. That this eventually became evident to the managers of such funds is obvious in the makeup of their portfolios today.

Chemical Fund is now a broadly diversified fund with only 20% of its assets in the chemical industry. Television Fund, which came out in 1948 when everyone was wild about the TV industry, turned into Television-Electronics Fund a few years later when the big growth mania switched from TV to electronics. When this bubble burst too, the fund changed to Technology Fund and is now a routinely diversified fund.

GO NORTH, YOUNG MAN

Back in the mid-1950s a boom in U.S. demand for Canadian stocks—mostly oil, gas, and uranium—spawned several funds, two of which are alive today even though they have never done much for their holders: Canadian Fund and Scudder International. Lesser fads have carried such bizarre groups as swimming pool makers, outboard motors, and bowling pinsetters to dizzying heights before invariably letting them plummet to disaster. The big fad of the early 1970s was, of course, gold and gold-mining shares, but more about that in Chapter 15.

YOU CAN'T GET RICH IN A HURRY

There have been other waves of popularity for ideas as well as particular industry groups. The most recent of these was "performance," or aggressive portfolio management. This meant moving rapidly from stock to stock, buying the trend rather than value, outguessing the market and the other fellow rather than security analysis, and seeking the new and dynamic while discarding the old and familiar. Obviously, performance was simply speculation by another name.

A ROSE BY ANY OTHER NAME . . .

The performance mania pervaded all of Wall Street and most of Main Street, but was easiest to see in the mutual fund business. After all, performance was about all one fund could boast about over another. Why would an investor swap his prestigious Massachusetts Investors Growth Stock Fund for the shares of a brand new and bumptious Mates Fund if it were not in the hope of getting rich faster?

The new and smaller funds promised more, and quicker. When Gerald Tsai first offered his untried and untested Manhattan Fund shares he got around $500 million almost overnight. Mr. Tsai's promise was simple—performance. Just as the public thought they had found a safe route to something for nothing, many professional managers had convinced themselves that they had exactly that to offer. Investment committees and research were out. Individual genius and market timing were in.

. . . SMELLS AS SWEET

Turnover soared. Where established funds had a history of 10%–20% portfolio turnover in a year, the new, alert managements of the "go-go" funds boasted turnover nine or ten times as great. Of the top 300 funds in 1968, 17 turned their portfolios over by 100%, 5 ran over 200%, and 2 exceeded 300%! Clearly, while the low-turnover old-line funds were trying to invest their shareholders' money, the new boys were simply playing a numbers game.

A glance at the stocks held in these portfolios would further

confirm this analysis. While Xerox, Atlantic Richfield, and Burroughs dominated the old-line holdings, new issues, letter stock,
and total unknowns characterized the frenetic end of the fund
spectrum.

Mutual fund managers weren't the only ones to throw conventional caution to the winds in the pursuit of the will-o'-the-wisp of
something for nothing. Portfolio managers for insurance companies, pension and profit-sharing funds, and college endowments
got the bug, too. Even the lofty Ford Foundation urged all
educational institutions to take a more aggressive stance in the
investment of endowment funds—meaning, don't be so cautious if
it is someone else's money.

Then came 1969, and an old lesson was relearned. There was
no "Northwest Passage" to instant riches. The route was still long
and roundabout. The go-go funds collapsed, some into the arms
of the SEC. Conglomerates became but shadows of their former
quotations. Heavily courted franchise and computer-leasing
stocks became old maids overnight. And the whole market went
about the repeal of the entire decade of the 1960s.

WAS NOTHING SACRED?

But all wasn't lost—not for the good growth stocks that represented sound products for expanding markets. Where the values
were, prices held. Consider the drug and hospital supply companies. Their shares dipped but didn't collapse. Holders of American Home Products, American Hospital Supply, and Warner-
Lambert had nothing to fear but fear itself. Burroughs and
Eastman Kodak stood their ground with a host of other solid
growth issues, reflecting the basic uptrend in their earning power.

And so it will always be—where stock prices are based on the
underlying values of assets and earning power, the risks in common stock ownership will be low and the probability of eventual
profits high. But when stock prices are based on turnover, hope,
and furious trading, the day of reckoning cannot be far off.

So resist the siren call of "something for nothing" that always proves so irresistible for the crowd on Wall Street. Be content to grow rich slowly, and mostly alone. There is no other way.

DIVERSIFY OR BUST

Rule number five is to diversify. Someone once said that the way to make money is to put all your eggs in one basket and then watch that basket like a hawk. Whoever said such a thing was half right. If you put everything into one stock and it soars, so will your fortunes. The corollary is, of course, that if the stock plummets instead, your fortunes vanish. So if you are bound to try the one-basket approach, be sure the company is one you know thoroughly and that it is operating in an industry you know equally well. Then plan to follow that company and the industry daily.

If you do all of this you may win, or lose, for luck is still very much part of the game. Too many things can happen that no amount of research will see in advance. Take Equity Funding, for instance. How would the best analyst in the world know that the company was manufacturing bogus insurance policies? After all, the company's financial reports had the seal of approval from perfectly respectable Seidman & Seidman, a California accounting firm.

The stories of people who used Equity Funding as their basket are heartrending, as well as legion. One was a 70-year-old New York lady, retired, living in a tiny apartment. She put her all, $7,000, in Equity Funding. When the company went down she lost her life savings, the result of 55 years of work, and found herself slowly sliding toward welfare. Her social security would not even pay her rent.

Across the Hudson River, an elderly father refused to retire despite his failing health. His wife and son could not understand, and he could not bring himself to tell them that his retirement fund was gone. He had put his $25,000 into 9.5% Equity Funding bonds and it was all gone.

A Nebraska couple borrowed on their assets and bought Equity

Funding common in the hope that the fast-rising price of this wonder stock would turn a few dollars into a lot. Then they planned to use the lot to buy their college-age son some medical attention that they otherwise could not afford. When the bubble broke, their hopes vanished. You can imagine their feelings when they faced the job of telling their boy why they could not get him the medical help he needed.

OVER AND OVER

So it goes, on and on. These sad stories are not new. On the contrary, people have been losing their shirts in one sort of market or another since the scores were kept on clay tablets. Don't you be one of them. Spread your risks by buying stock in more than one company.

Even if you have only a little bit, diversify. This can be done by buying more than one stock, by investing in broadly diversified industrial companies (see page 172), or by going the mutual fund route. Whichever way you do diversify, you will be condemning yourself to an "average" experience. You will miss the thrill of instant riches. But so also will you likely avoid sudden financial disaster. As one of your stock selections sinks, some other will probably soar, leaving you, on average, in pretty good shape.

And while you are diversifying in a number of companies, you should also spread your investments over a number of different industries. They all should be promising industries. Don't buy into a dead-end field just to diversify. If this practice pulls your portfolio performance down to a dull level of mediocrity, console yourself that you can sleep nights.

FIVE GOOD RULES

We can pause here to sum up our rules for investing:

1. Decide what you want your savings to do for you before you plunge.

2. Buy the best-known companies.
3. Invest for the long term. Patience with the stock market is more than a virtue. It's a must.
4. Avoid fads. Stay clear of the crowd, even when it looks right.
5. Diversify. Few "sure things" prove as sure as they seem.

5

How to Buy Growth Stocks

In the first four chapters of this book we dealt with a few basic rules that should govern any investment program. The first was to know what you want your dollars to do for you. Do you want income now, or growth tomorrow, or something in between? Let's assume now that growth is what you want.

Although extra income is always a delight, you don't really *need* it and, way down the road, you will retire someday. Money put aside now will be a lifesaver then. If it can be made to multiply in the meantime, all the better.

That being the case, how does one invest for growth? How does one tell a growth stock from any other? Where does one look for them? This process is not nearly as difficult as it might seem. Actually, if you are willing to spend just a little time, it is downright easy. Here's the way you do it.

First, think of the areas in which our economy is growing most. What phases of life are most discussed in the daily paper? It's energy—there's a shortage of gas and heating oil. It's pollution control—there are blobs of oil at midocean and the air even over Phoenix is dirty. It's leisure time—what was the big issue in the 1973 Chrysler strike? It was not money. It was overtime. The

United Auto Workers wanted voluntary overtime because many of the employees preferred leisure time to extra pay.

There is also tremendous growth going on in services, health, technology, science, and, oddly enough, retailing. On the other hand, there is relatively little growth going on in our major old-line industries such as steel, autos, chemicals, and paper. Part of this reflects a change in the times. Steel used to be the basis of life, at least business and industrial life, when we were building an industrial society and supplying manufactured goods to the rest of the world. But now we, and they, have plenty of those things. Now we want medical research so we can live longer, or longer vacations so we can travel more.

This puts the steel industry in the position of growing along with gross national product—just a few percentage points each year—and some years there is no growth at all. If growth of sales or revenues slows, growth in earnings very nearly vanishes. And when earnings growth goes, price-earnings ratios plummet. This is why the prices of shares are so low in relation to earnings for such industry giants as Grace (5 times), FMC (6 times), Continental Can (9 times), and NL Ind. (5 times) while the Dow-Jones Industrial Average sells at an average 10 times at this writing and good growth stocks at two or three times that level.

HARD WORK AND NO PLAY . . .

Let's look at some of the growth areas in more detail. Take leisure time, where a real revolution has occurred. "Here it is Monday noon already, tomorrow's Tuesday, the next day's Wednesday. The week is almost half over and we have yet to get in a day's work." So Ma greeted the hands down on the farm at the turn of the century. Our country was built on this tradition for hard work. The heavy labor necessary for survival was also good in itself. It was the Puritan ethic and it was new to mankind. It has persisted until fairly recently. Plenty of people alive today remember working a 12-hour day. Anyone over 50 can recall Saturday morning at the office. If you worked hard, you got a two-week vacation.

. . . WILL GET JACK INTO HEAVEN

Ancient Rome and Athens, on the other hand, rated leisure the prime objective of civilized man. As recently as the start of the Industrial Revolution men and women had to be forced into the factories of the English Midlands. Even the Russian peasant, toil-worn in legend, labored only in summer, spending his long winter almost completely at leisure.

We may not move all the way back to those days of extreme free time, but we certainly are traveling in that direction. The two-week vacation, once the goal of millions, is now the minimum for two thirds of the 85 million people working. According to the National Association of Business Economists, paid vacations jumped 50% in the 1950s. The boom in leisure hours stemmed from an average annual productivity increase of 3%, even though part was taken in dollars, by moonlighting, and only part in actual time off.

And the trend is toward more free hours, time off, rather than extra dollars. This reflects the more carefree younger workers and the growing number of older workers whose modest living costs make leisure hours more appealing than extra income. In fact, it is primarily the middle-aged who still prefer dollars, for they are the ones so saddled with tuition payments, orthodontists, and wedding parties that time off is a luxury they cannot yet afford.

WORK—A THING OF THE PAST?

From 1900 to 1960 life expectancy for men gained 18 years, time on the job only 9 years, leaving 9 years to "play." The figures for women are 22 and 14, leaving them ahead by 8. Given further gains in life expectancy, future increases in productivity comparable with the 3% annual rate of the past two decades, plus the growing appeal of time off over extra income, we are sure to see earlier retirements and a shorter workweek in the years immediately ahead. We could have a 20-hour four-day week by 1990 and still support a level GNP, or we could stick to 40 hours and five days and retire at 38, also with a level GNP. Either way, the United States has stumbled on a cornucopia of leisure hours which means, among many other things, rapidly expanding new markets for snowmobiles and surfboards, golf clubs and skis, retirement homes and vacation villas, and exhausting trips to Lisbon, La Paz, and, of course, Disneyland.

Thus, the companies listed as follows serve these needs and seem inevitably bound to grow.

American Express, a bank, adviser, and home-away-from-home for all but the most sophisticated traveler. Long a leader in travelers' checks, the company has moved with the times into credit cards, mutual funds, insurance, and travel agencies.

AMF Inc. has moved from missiles and bomb casings to motorcycles, bicycles, golf clubs, sailboats, and snowmobiles.

Brunswick Corp. is strong in outboard motors, bowling, fishing reels, and golf equipment. This company is also well represented in the rapidly growing medical supplies area.

Coleman Co., as a supplier of the do-it-yourself traveler, has long been the big name in camping, and is now producing for the growing mobile home market.

Disney (Walt), with the biggest man-made attraction in the West, has now done it again in Florida with Disney World.

Howard Johnson operates in 40 states, Washington, D.C., Puerto Rico, the Bahamas, and Canada. With gasoline again in plentiful supply, Americans, along with most people in the western world, can be expected to "take to the road" once again with enthusiasm, all to the benefit of "HoJo."

	EARNINGS PER SHARE		Dec. 1975 Price	P/E Ratio	1975 Dividend	Yield
	1975	1974				
American Express	$2.50	$2.18	39	16	$ .80	2.1%
AMF, Inc.	1.85	1.19	21	11	1.24	5.9
Brunswick Corp.	1.10	2.06	12	11	.40	3.3
Coleman Co.	.85	.48	12	14	.44	3.7
Disney (Walt)	2.00	1.63	49	25	.12*	0.2
Howard Johnson	1.00	.81	15	15	.24	1.6
Outboard Marine	2.42	2.02	28	12	1.20	4.3

* Plus stock.

Outboard Marine makes Johnson and Evinrude outboard motors, plus snowmobiles, camper trailers, golf carts, chain saws, and lawn-care equipment.

SERVICE IS THE THING

There are all sorts of services you can buy today. Things you can get others to do for you that you would rather *not* do for yourself. You can hire people now to protect you from thieves, do your tax returns, clean your house, exterminate your mice, and wash your clothes—not to mention someone like United Business Service to manage your money!

With every passing year a constantly *smaller* percentage of our working population must "man their machines" in order to keep us clothed, fed, housed, automobiled, and televisioned. Services passed manufacturing in total employment in 1957, and their value in dollars exceeded that of manufacturing in 1965. In the past ten years alone, employment in service industries climbed 72% while manufacturing jobs crept ahead a modest 25%.

There are a number of good companies in the various service areas, all of which have had excellent growth records. What's more, there is every reason to believe that their growth in the future will be every bit as good. Here are a representative few:

Allied Maintenance is 60% in janitorial work and 40% in fueling and parts storage for airports, both here and in Canada.

American District Telegraph will protect your valuables (whatever and wherever they are) with electronic monitoring devices.

H & R Block is the biggest thing in doing tax returns. Growth has been of whirlwind proportions.

Rollins derives almost two thirds of sales from exterminating any sort of pest you have. Termites, roaches, rats, and even invisible bacteria are no match for this company.

Servisco manufactures, rents, sells, and launders work clothes. To a much lesser degree the company is also in building maintenance and security guard service.

	EARNINGS PER SHARE		Dec. 1975 Price	P/E Ratio	1975 Dividend	Yield
	1975	1974				
Allied Maintenance	$1.65	$1.70	11	7	$.60	5.5%
American District Telegraph	2.20	2.08	24	11	.56	2.3
H & R Block	1.58	1.29	16	10	.80	5.0
Rollins Inc.	1.42	1.26	23	16	.30	1.3
Servisco	.14	.62	3	21	.30	10.0

HEALTH COMES FIRST

Another major area of future growth is health. According to The Conference Board, an economic and business research organization, national expenditures for health care rose from $78.35 to $394.16 per person between 1950 and 1972. The same board estimates national outlays on research construction and personal health care will rise to $780.02 per capita by 1980—and that isn't very far away!

It will come as no surprise to most Americans to learn that medical care prices rose at an average annual rate of 3.9% in the 1950s, 4.7% in the 1960s, and 6.5% in the early 1970s versus 2.1%, 2.7%, and 4.3%, respectively, for consumer goods. This disparity reflects the cost of major medical advances—research and development on new ways to keep our old bodies going longer, if not forever.

These trends will likely continue. Thus, purveyors of services and supplies to the health industry should continue to prosper. The hospital supply business is part of this, obviously. So also are the drug companies. Some of the greatest growth records of the postwar years are in these two phases of the health business.

Hospital chains are a newer and chancier part of the industry. These chains are privately owned facilities operated for profit—in marked contrast to the usual local community hospital run by, for, and at the expense of, the community.

The private sector of the industry now accounts for about 7% of the nation's hospital beds. The growth potential is good but the risks are higher than in drugs or supplies because (1) there are enough beds, with actual excess capacity in some areas; (2) the average length of hospital stays is in a steady downtrend (hospital charges are so high that only the desperately ill can face them!); (3) the flow of federal funds to hospitals and medical care generally has slowed.

However, the high-profit areas—such auxiliary services as lab tests and X-rays—are growing rapidly, despite the shorter hospital stay of the average patient. Thus, overall prospects for the better chains remain excellent.

Other areas of growth in the health industry are in the optical, dental, and diagnostic equipment field. To give an idea of the volume of dollars likely to flow into these areas, note that the 1973 Chrysler contract settlement included a dental care program, to start in the fall of 1975. At the end of three years the plan will be almost entirely paid for by the employers with the costs coming out of the cost-of-living allowance ordinarily payable in cash to the workers. In other words, the union traded part of a cost-of-living adjustment to obtain "free" dental care—forever and ever. If this becomes an industrial pattern, think of the literally billions of new dollars that will flow into dentistry!

Aside from these areas, the fast pace of health care technology itself offers exciting growth potential for investors. So does the fact that in the aggregate, we're living longer. A representative program in health should look like this:

Abbott Laboratories, one of the world's leading hospital suppliers, and also important in drugs.

American Home Products is about the largest producer of drugs, both proprietary (those you can buy off the shelf) and ethical (those that require a prescription).

American Hospital Supply is the unquestioned industry leader in the supply area, with an impressive growth record. Hence, the extremely high P/E (see table).

Baxter Laboratories is big in artificial human "parts," medical technology generally, and supplies.

Damon is a leader in diagnostic equipment, lab tests, and related technology.

Hospital Corporation of America is one of the better-managed chains with a well-executed program of growth through internal expansion and acquisitions. Operating largely in the South, the company has expanded from one hospital in 1968 to 51 units, 7,500 beds, and $200 million in revenues in 1974.

Pfizer turned 100 years old in 1949 and promptly entered the fastest growth period of its existence. Growth has come largely from excellent internal research and development, making the company an international giant.

Warner-Lambert is another major growth factor in the drug industry. But in addition, the stock also gives investors a toehold in dental care, a sizable foothold in the optical world through wholly owned American Optical Co., and, if you can stand it, a position in chewing gum plus cough medicine and antacids through American Chicle, also a subsidiary.

	EARNINGS PER SHARE		Dec. 1975 Price	P/E Ratio	1975 Dividend	Yield
	1975	1974				
Abbott Laboratories	$2.50	$2.00	41	16	$.80	2.0%
American Home Products	1.55	1.42	37	24	.92	2.4
American Hospital Supply	1.45	1.28	34	23	.34	0.9
Baxter Laboratories	1.40	1.22	42	30	.19	0.5
Damon	.27	1.17	9	33	.20	2.2
Hospital Corp. of America	2.25	1.73	24	11	.24	1.0
Pfizer	2.15	1.93	28	13	.81	2.9
Warner-Lambert	2.20	1.98	37	17	.92	2.5

AFTER OIL, THE ATOM

Probably few citizens view the burgeoning nuclear power age with complete equanimity. Thinking along "what if" lines comes easily and conjures up apocalyptic visions. Also, natural fears of the man in the street continue to be fanned by a variety of environmentalists who stoutly oppose every advance of the atom. And progress proceeds at a snail's pace due to supercautious procedures.

Despite this, the long-term outlook for manufacturers in this field is excellent. Oil and gas are in short supply, and coal must overcome certain pollution and cost drawbacks. Nuclear power is the logical answer, especially for needs in the 1980s and beyond, when the fast breeder reactor (which produces more fuel than it consumes) should be available. Atomic power now provides only 7% of U.S. electricity requirements, but the percentage seems certain to rise sharply in the 1980s.

Investing in nuclear power is somewhat difficult because no company is wholly in it, except perhaps for some uranium mining companies. But even in the mining end of the business it is not easy to get a "pure" investment. Gulf Oil, for example, has immense uranium reserves in Canada and is a leading developer of the high-temperature, gas-cooled nuclear reactor which is rapidly gaining converts due to environmental advantages and capital economies.

In looking for growth in nuclear development, therefore, one has to consider uranium producers or equipment suppliers. There isn't much glory likely for the electric utility companies using nuclear reactors. It just means an alternate fuel which may or may not help earnings. In the producing group one finds such companies as Denison Mines Ltd. and Rio Algom, both Canadian concerns. In the United States, United Nuclear and Kerr-McGee lead.

	EARNINGS PER SHARE		Dec. 1975 Price	P/E Ratio	1975 Divi- dend	Yield
	1975	1974				
Denison Mines	$4.03	$2.69	51	13	$2.00	3.9%
Kerr–McGee	5.15	4.64	72	14	1.00	1.3
Reserve Oil & Minerals	.39	.26	7	18	Nil	Nil
United Nuclear	.55	.08	14	25	Nil	Nil

Until quite recently, the uranium business has been in the doldrums. Prices—and earnings, therefore—have been depressed by an oversupply. But within the past year or two, uranium prices have tripled and per-share profits have responded accordingly. The shares of uranium producers have understandably performed better than the market as a whole.

While the present picture is well above average, the long pull seems inevitably better. We must lessen our dependence on oil, and nuclear power has to be one of the answers. As nuclear power plants open up, uranium demand should rise and push prices to better levels. As this develops, these four producers, among others, should continue to prosper.

Among the equipment suppliers are a couple of industry leaders that everyone has heard of, General Electric and Westinghouse Electric, and a trio you may not be quite familiar with, Babcock & Wilcox, Combustion Engineering, and Foster Wheeler.

General Electric officials are convinced that nuclear power is *the* energy source of the future. Management is committing considerable manpower and resources (over $60 million annually) to expanding the firm's already sizable nuclear capabilities. As 1974 drew to a close the total number of GE nuclear plants built or on order approximated 102 units (over 23 abroad), with a combined capacity of more than 70 million kilowatts. Total company backlogs exceed $19 billion—some $12 billion in the power generation area, and more than $4 billion of that for nuclear equipment. Nuclear business is now growing profitably at GE and, as these massive backlogs are worked down, should make an increasingly greater contribution.

Westinghouse, with about 40% of the nuclear market at home and 50% in Europe, is well situated to serve this growing industry. While the frantic order pace of recent years has slowed—in part, no doubt, due to the unfavorable publicity about its fuel rod problems (since solved)—Westinghouse has enough business booked (over $3 billion) to keep it busy for the rest of this decade. This includes prime responsibility for designing and building the nation's first large-scale demonstration fast breeder reactor, and work on four platform-mounted power stations (costing about $350 million each) for Public Service Company of New Jersey.

Babcock & Wilcox derived 78% of 1972 sales from steam generating and related equipment, 16% from tubular products, and the balance from refractories and machine tools, etc. Loss of market share in the fossil field and nuclear development costs produced a lean period in 1969 and 1970. However, earnings moved sharply higher in the following two years as the company regained its former 40% slice of total steam generating system sales, and earlier large nuclear losses finally ended. Demand is strong for nuclear fuel and components, fossil systems, and tubular products. B & W appears to have a viable nuclear position, and its traditional business is good.

Combustion Engineering has fared extremely well as a leading maker of fossil-fueled steam generating equipment and appears headed for further success in the nuclear field. Sales of generating equipment to utility and industrial customers accounted for 49% of 1972 income before taxes and overhead. Earnings climbed 270% between 1962 and 1972 with only one backward step (in 1968). CE received the largest nuclear order ever given in 1973 when Duke Power signed a $200 million contract for six nuclear power plants and the enriched uranium needed for their reactors. Another $100 million in nuclear orders followed from two other utilities.

Foster Wheeler's profits are split fairly evenly between processing plants and steam generating equipment. A nuclear department was established in 1970, and a planned facility to manufacture nuclear power plant components (jointly owned with a subsidiary of Gulf Oil) is scheduled to be operating in Florida in 1974. Long-term prospects are also bright for the company's oil and synthetic natural gas processing business and for its various pollution control products. Processing work is normally cyclical, but present world energy requirements provide a very encouraging background.

POLLUTION, POLLUTION EVERYWHERE

One of the shocking discoveries of recent years was that economic growth is not all good, for it produces pollution. In fact, the greater the economic growth of a nation, whether industrial or agricultural, the greater the pollution. The consumption of energy, the transformation of materials into finished goods, the movement of those goods and people, the spreading of fertilizer to speed the growth of food and fiber—all cause pollution.

The once idyllic city of Los Angeles disappeared in a lung-searing smog years ago. The crystalline air of Phoenix and Denver took on the hues of Newark and Buffalo. Japan, whose growth from 1950 to the 1970s broke all records, ran abruptly into the pollution problem when a number of citizens died from eating fish taken from ocean waters fouled with industrial wastes. The Russians faced their share of ecological agony as paper mills began to sour Lake Baikal, the world's deepest lake and the largest body of fresh water in Eurasia.

But pollution can be licked. Pittsburgh did it first in the late 1940s and early 1950s. London did it in the 1960s. All it takes is money, and when money is spent to clean things up, some of that money will stick to the companies that make the equipment and do the work. The stocks of such companies have turned in a roller-coaster performance in recent years, reflecting our enthusiasm at the start when the needs for pollution control were "discovered" and later dismay when legislation, federal funding, and enforcement seemed to waver.

Nevertheless, pollution control is here to stay and some stockholders are sure to prosper. Our candidates for such are the following:

American Air Filter has about $250 million sales, with three basic product areas: filtration of intake air; air pollution control (perhaps 35% of sales); and air conditioning, heating, and ventilating. In the pollution control field, the firm is especially notable for wet scrubbers and fabric filter systems; its first full-scale sulfur dioxide scrubber system began operating in late 1975.

Combustion Equipment Associates' sales are divided thus: 49% industrial pollution control (incinerators, scrubbers, fuel from solid waste); 25% additional lines involving pollution control (automatic combustion systems, commercial incinerators, instrumentation, and waste compactors); 17% materials handling and processing equipment; and 13% farm machinery parts.

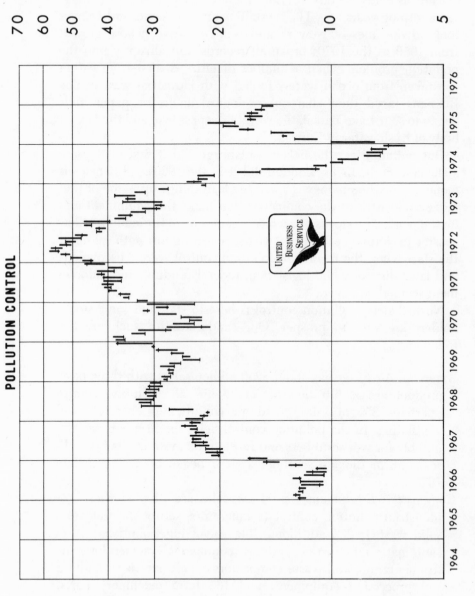

POLLUTION CONTROL

Data source: Standard & Poor's. Used by permission.

There are three notable installations coming on stream: a major sulfur dioxide system at an electric power plant, a municipal incinerator and recycling plant, and a large industrial pollution control facility. In the latter two instances, CEA has long-term contracts to operate the facilities.

Envirotech was formed in 1969 with this game plan: acquisitions of firms well established in liquids-solids separation (for water and waste water treatment and continuous process industries); expansion from this base to other environmental areas; and maintaining sound finances and at least a 15% annual growth rate in earnings per share. Sales are about 61% liquids-solids business (with world dominance in water pollution control); 17% air pollution control (all areas including work on sulfur dioxide); and 22% tunneling and mining equipment (a fast-growing business acquired as part of the big Eimco liquids-solids operation). Earnings growth since 1969 has averaged more than 20% a year.

Peabody-Galion's sales are divided about 24% air pollution control (especially strong in combustion systems and wet scrubbers, including developmental systems for sulfur dioxide removal); 20% water pollution control (best known for sewage pumps and aeration systems); 14% solid wastes management (industry leadership in refuse trucks, compactors, and transfer stations); 12% pollution control services (engineering, monitoring, testing, leasing, etc.); 10% other services, largely related to energy fields; and 20% truck equipment and other lines. The business is well balanced, and earnings growth is better than 10% annually.

Research-Cottrell has long been dominant in electrostatic precipitators, and in recent years has also diversified substantially. We estimate sales about as follows: 25% precipitators; 23% other air pollution business (mainly fabric filters and wet scrubbers, also other lines, including auto exhaust catalysts); 19% environmental engineering (about 70% related to waste water systems and solid waste disposal); 17% tall chimneys; and 16% cooling towers. Easing of sulfur dioxide standards is helping the chimney business, and R-C itself is exploring three approaches to sulfur dioxide control.

Zurn Industries has sales of somewhat over $235 million, classified by management at roughly 58% environmental products and services, 32% energy systems, and 10% leisure products. The so-called environmental group actually includes many things other than pollution control. However, Zurn does have a broad range of products and services involving air, water, and solid waste pollution control.

	EARNINGS PER SHARE		Price Range 1974–75	Dec. 1975 Price	P/E Ratio	1975 Dividend
	1975	1974				
American Air Filter	$1.75	$1.32	22–6	15	9	$.48
Combustion Equipment Assoc.	1.56	1.42	25–6	14	9	Nil
Envirotech Corp.	2.00	1.70	35–8	18	9	Nil
Peabody-Galion	1.60	1.48	31–8	15	9	.08
Research-Cottrell	.01	.77	44–4	15	–	.08
Zurn Industries	1.00	.83	13–4	9	9	.32

6

More on Growth

Partly related to the companies discussed in the preceding chapter but also partly separate are what can loosely be called the high technology companies. These are companies that operate with highly sophisticated equipment, spend huge sums on research and development, and often relate to human rather than industrial needs.

One group that particularly fits the above are the so-called instrumentation companies. Their efforts are in the complex instrumentation required for hospital laboratories, cancer research, pollution analysis and control, mass transit control (note San Francisco's BART trains which are controlled by computers rather than train crews), etc. Because these areas meet human needs directly, the growth potentials are limitless. Yet because they function at the outer edge of human experience and knowledge, their earnings records are bound to be spotty. Sometimes they win, sometimes they don't. Their shares, therefore, are moderately speculative. In this group we include such companies as Perkin-Elmer, Hewlett-Packard, General Signal, and Foxboro.

Another technology group that may not meet the human-related characteristic quite as well but are nevertheless in a dynamic growth area are the electric data-processing people—the computer makers. Modern life would not be possible as we have come to know it without the computer and allied data-processing equipment. The future will be even more dependent on these machines that can do anything (but think!) better and infinitely faster and more accurately than the brightest humans. But this is obvious. Everyone knows the stocks to buy to participate—IBM, Burroughs, Sperry Rand, and Digital Equipment.

A third part of the high technology area is electronics—particularly the semiconductors, which are the heart of all sorts of miniaturized circuitry. This is the least stable part of the high technology field. It is more cyclical in nature as intense demand encourages overbuilding and subsequently overcapacity, price cutting, and sharply lower earnings. Then growing demand eventually soaks up the extra capacity, competition abates, prices recover, and earnings bounce back in time to finance a new series of capacity increases, which leads to yet another downward cycle.

Nevertheless, while growth through the years has been irregular, it has been undeniably present, spurred by a steady flow of new and ever more sophisticated electronic devices that today are sometimes no bigger than the head of a small pin. Semiconductor products (tiny printed circuits used in most electrical devices) made possible the birth of minicomputers and minicalculators. More and more color TVs being built today are all solid-state. These miniature devices will also be found in more automobiles, appliances, office equipment, and even in your wrist watch. The industry's last period of fits and starts occurred in the late 1960s. However, pent-up demand and a surging economy rescued many of these companies in the 1972–73 period. Also, worldwide demand for many electronics products has far outstripped domestic demand in recent years. The markets outside our shores for color TVs, computers, automobiles, farm machinery, etc., far from saturated, provide hopes that overall growth will continue at above-average rates, at least into the mid-1980s. All this is in spite of the experience of an economic slowdown in 1974, both here and abroad—thanks mostly to the petroleum pinch, not to mention double-digit inflation.

Many an electronics concern today is scurrying just to get enough business to keep things humming. The 1973–75 recession largely eliminated order backlogs. Nevertheless, inventories are unusually low, despite slack demand, and there has not been the overbuilding of capacity that was the bane of past such cycles. Thus, prospects for the industry are good.

As with the market generally, there is a two-tier market for electronic stocks. The favorites like Texas Instruments, Perkin-Elmer, and Hewlett-Packard offer the minimum risk in the group. There are a number of excellently managed, well-rounded concerns selling at reasonable prices for those who can take a modest chance. We refer particularly to issues like Raytheon, Varian, Wang, Lear Siegler, Microwave, and EG&G. All have strong earnings potential and yet the market has tended to neglect them, preferring the industry leaders, although even these are hardly overbid. For the investor who can stand a roller-coaster ride, this industry has appeal.

	EARNINGS PER SHARE		Price Range 1974–75	Dec. 1975 Price	P/E Ratio	1975 Divi- dend
	1975	1974				
Burroughs Corp.	$3.95	$3.66	113–61	84	21	$ .60
EG&G	1.15	.97	20–7	14	12	.14
Foxboro	3.30	2.02	48–19	29	9	.80
General Signal	3.25	2.71	53–17	37	11	.84
Hewlett-Packard	3.05	3.08	121–52	96	31	.31
IBM	12.85	12.47	254–151	224	17	7.00
Lear Siegler	1.30	1.17	9–3	6	5	.32
Micro-Wave Assoc.	1.90	1.92	27–8	14	7	Nil
Perkin-Elmer	1.08	.98	40–15	25	23	.28
Raytheon Co.	4.75	3.85	60–20	46	10	1.00
Sperry Rand	3.90	3.81	49–23	40	10	.76
Texas Instruments	2.70	3.92	119–59	94	35	1.00
Varian Associates	1.10	1.08	19–5	14	13	.20
Wang Laboratories	.80	1.20	20–6	10	13	.10

GROWTH IN THE HUMDRUM

One doesn't often think of the retail business when looking for long-term growth. To most of us retail means the local department store, the drugstore on the corner, or perhaps the A&P. But romantic or no, the retail boys have been building volume and

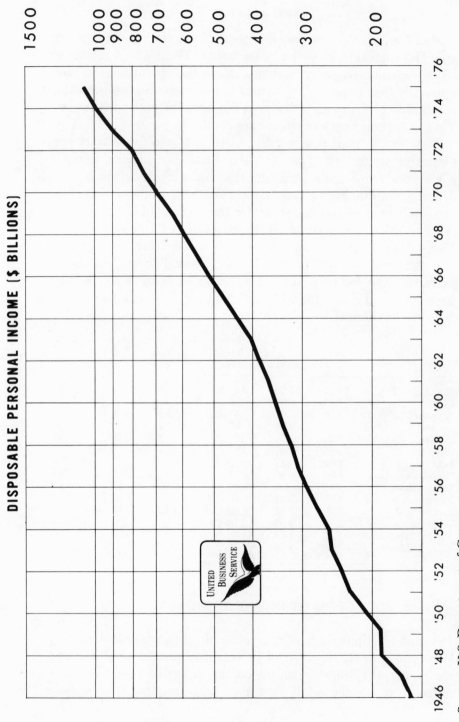

DISPOSABLE PERSONAL INCOME ($ BILLIONS)

1500 1000 900 800 700 600 500 400 300 200

1946 '48 '50 '52 '54 '56 '58 '60 '62 '64 '66 '68 '70 '72 '74 '76

UNITED
BUSINESS
SERVICE

Source: U.S. Department of Commerce

profits in an almost unconscionable fashion since the troops came home in 1945.

This experience does not reflect the genius of the leaders in the industry half so much as it does the national conviction that there ought to be a job for everyone. Thus, Congress passed the Full Employment Act in 1946 which made sure that personal income would go only one way—up.

EMPLOYMENT ACT OF 1946

The Congress declares that it is the continuing policy and responsibility of the Federal Government to use all practicable means . . . for the purpose of creating and maintaining . . . conditions under which there will be afforded useful employment opportunities . . . for those able, willing and seeking to work, and to promote maximum employment, production, and purchasing power.

The chart on page 64 shows what happened as a result. Disposable personal income, the dollars available for spending, rose steadily year after year, regardless of boom or recession, for a quarter of a century. This was a first for mankind.

The average per year advance of disposable personal income was 6.9% during the 1950s and 9.6% during the 1960s. These figures compared with an average annual rise in the cost of living of 2.2% and 2.6%, respectively. Even in 1974 when the inflationary surge was at its worst, disposable personal income advanced by 10%, more than enough to top the highest annual jump in the cost of living in a generation.

Meantime, consumers demonstrated their infinite appetite for things by regularly spending 92%–94% of their disposable income. Small wonder, then, that retail sales swelled across the land, taking profits of the big and little alike through the roof again and again. But then, all retailers did not fare identically in this flood of consumer spending. The better managed and better situated outdid the rest. Such can be seen easily in the statistical table on page 66.

RETAILING

	Quality Rating*	Dec. 1975 Price	1975 Earn- ings	EARNINGS GAINS PER YEAR 1974– 1975	1971– 1974	P/E Ratio	Divi- dend
Albertson Inc.	M	24	$2.25	22%	30%	11	$ .60
Dillon Cos.	M	30	1.97	29	32	15	.96
Eckerd (Jack)	M	26	1.32	10	32	20	.36
Edison Bros. Stores	M	48	5.00	22	24	10	1.48
Heck's Inc.	S	14	1.75	5	16	8	.16
House of Fabrics	S	11	.90	20	14	12	.20
Kresge (S.S.)	H	34	1.30	49	12	26	.24
Longs Drug Stores	M	67	2.75	20	18	24	.80
Lucky Stores	M	17	1.25	11	9	14	.64†
Melville Shoe	M	18	1.60	48	6	11	.48
Mercantile Stores	M	57	4.50	26	9	13	.80
Pay 'n Save	S	26	2.05	21	38	13	.30
Petrie Stores	S	72	3.26	13	28	22	1.00
Rite Aid	S	15	.91	36	13	16	.16
Safeway Stores	H	44	4.90	60	5	9	2.00
Sears Roebuck	H	71	3.00	8	11	24	1.85
Southland Corp.	M	23	1.89	11	16	13	.40
Unity Buying Service	S	13	1.80	7	38	7	Nil
Wal-Mart Stores	S	15	.56	17	36	27	.08
Winn-Dixie Stores	H	38	2.69	7	15	14	1.44

* H–high; M–medium; S–speculative.
† Plus stock.

Note particularly the columns headed, "Earnings gains per year." This is a very important measure of corporate growth. See how they vary; e.g., 38% each year 1971–74 for Wal-Mart and 11% per year for Sears Roebuck. However, earnings growth is not the only measure. Other things have to be considered. For example, how could Sears Roebuck, with sales of more than $13 billion, be expected to grow as fast as a much smaller company with sales of a mere $240 million? There are variations in risk involved, too. Sears, as we all know, is a household word, while Wal-Mart is a relatively new discount chain on the West Coast.

However, what we are illustrating here is that there can be growth in "unexciting" areas of the economy. To find these, you generally need the figures expressed in the foregoing retailing table and a little "horse sense" in their evaluation.

THINGS TO LOOK OUT FOR

Lastly, one shouldn't present a peroration such as this on growth stocks without some warning about price-earnings ratios—excessive ones, that is. When a blue-chip growth stock favorite such as American Hospital Supply, IBM, or Xerox gets to a P/E of 40, 50, or 60 times, one should pause, particularly when the market as a whole is selling at 12 or 13 times, which it did through much of 1973.

Xerox is unquestionably a great company, but is it worth three times the average Dow-Jones share? One cannot be definite on this, but one can say that when a high-flying growth stock gets to the high side of its characteristic P/E, let someone else do the buying. When it gets down to midrange or less, you can pony up your dollars for a few shares.

Experience has shown that the best place to put your savings dollars, year in and year out, is in growth stocks. These are the shares of our leading corporations, the ones that will outgrow the economy and thereby give you a good slice of the future. If you can afford the immediate lack of dividends, you will be nicely rewarded in the end.

AUNT GLENDORA DID IT RIGHT

Let us illustrate this dictum with a case history—a true story. We had a friend who to us was the incarnation of the 1890s, even in the 1970s. Her name was Glendora, Aunt Glendora, and she was as proper and gentle and determined as any young lady who was born in 1878 would be.

After two years of normal school, Aunt Glendora became a schoolteacher, a profession she followed with single-minded devotion all her working life. (Oh, how Albert Shanker would have shocked her!) Teachers were not paid very much in Glendora's day, but her stern Puritanism was more than a match for the penury of impecunious school boards.

By 1931 her savings permitted an investment in Eastman Kodak. She bought 12 shares at $160 per, for $1,920. Thereafter, she kept every stock dividend, and when the company issued scrip for fractional shares, Aunt Glendora ponied up the required cash to get another full share. She was meticulous in records and even added in a flawless hand such commentaries as, "So I paid for 18 shares, and all the rest of my shares are stock dividends (not to be declared on income tax!) Besides, the cash dividend increased most years!"

Her Eastman Kodak cost a total of $3,272 for the original 12 shares plus the 18 she bought along the way. When Aunt Glendora departed this world, her investment in Eastman Kodak had grown to 856 shares and $110,000. One of Aunt Glendora's penned observations was, "You can see why I just keep still when [sister] Helen boasts of how wonderful that Torrington stock is."

So, there it is; buy the good ones and hang on.

BUT NEVER SELL? ? ?

Obviously, there are times and situations in which one should sell. When even Aunt Glendora should sell. There are two ways to look at the problem of selling—from the point of view of the market generally, and from the standpoint of the individual issue.

A fellow wrote in once and told me that he had finally figured out how to buy at the bottom and sell at the top. He determined the average bear market drop, 28%, and the average bull market rise, 77%, using the Dow-Jones Industrial Average. The following table shows how the figures look:

Low		% Decline	High		% Appreciation
1942	92.92	−39	1946	212.50	+129
1949	161.60	−24	1951	276.37	+71
1953	255.49	−8	1956	521.05	+104
1957	419.79	−19	1961	734.91	+75
1962	535.76	−27	1966	955.15	+86
1966	744.32	−25	1968	985.21	+32
1970	631.16	−36	1973	1051.70	+67
1974	570.00	−46	1975	881.81	+55
Average of bear markets		−28	Average of bull markets		+77

EASY DOES IT

It looks easy. If the average rise is 77%, sell out when the market is up that much. And when the subsequent decline occurs, jump in when the Dow is off the average 28%. Trouble is, working with averages means trouble. The average market decline is just as realistic as the 2.1 children per college-educated family. The market rarely does anything average. Just like the weather, the market is forever making new records.

Not only are major market turns impossible for mortals to pinpoint, but they do not always coincide with the market highs of your stocks. In the big 1973 decline the big growth stocks hardly trembled. It wasn't, in fact, until the oil embargo came along late in the year that the growth blue chips gave real ground, and by that time the decline in the Dow was nearly a year old.

A MARKET OF STOCKS

So when you get right down to it, valid generalizations on the stock market are tough to make. One is left with the study of individual common stocks. The stocks do represent companies which have assets and liabilities, sales and earnings, products and processes, and managements and employees.

You keep an eye on these companies, or pay an investment adviser to do it for you. And when things begin to slow down for them, you perk up for a closer look. If there is anything developing which makes them look less likely to grow and prosper—new competition, new laws, new products—sell your stock and use the money to buy something else, where the problems seem fewer and the prospects better.

There are many examples of this, but one of the best was Scott Paper, back in the 1960s. Scott was the foremost maker of premium tissue and toweling. The company's record was one of dynamic growth. The stock was a blue-chip growth favorite and sold at lofty price-earnings ratios. The company had a huge and growing market pretty much to itself.

Then Procter & Gamble moved in. They bought a midwestern outfit named Charmin (the don't-squeeze-it stuff) and took off after Scott's tissue and toweling customers. This shook the Scott management at the time. To have the expert marketers at P&G after your customers would scare anyone.

Here then was a perfect example of fundamental change. Scott went from being virtually alone in a rich market to being eyeball to eyeball with one of the world's toughest competitors. The market saw this and the Scott P/E tumbled. Investors then who sold were doing the right thing for logical reasons. The fundamentals at Scott had changed.

To sum up on selling: It's tough to do right. It should always be done with individual stock analysis for concrete reasons—never because you think you sense a major change for the worse in stock market values generally, unless, of course, you have a proven record in extrasensory perception or in just plain witchcraft.

7

Investing for Income

Back in Chapter 1 we showed how a working girl of "middle years" could buy stocks to provide income now. This is what many people need. They can't wait for tomorrow and for many good reasons shouldn't. There comes a point in everyone's life when tomorrow is so close it's almost today.

Selecting income stocks is easy. You look first for a business that is steady, as contrasted with cyclical. The machine tool companies, a feast-or-famine business if there ever was one, are a good example of the latter; the telephone business is a fair representative of the former. People tend to use the telephone as much in bad times as good. With the number of people and the level of popular affluence rising year after year, so should telephone revenues.

The only real problems the telephone business should have are from inflation and politics. The former pushes up costs, of both labor and capital (through higher interest rates). The politics comes in when the company seeks rate relief from the squeeze of rising costs. Lots of times the regulatory authorities think first of the consumer's reluctance to pay more for telephone service and second, if at all, of the stockholder's right to a fair return on his investment. After all, in the popular lexicon, the user is poor, the stockholder rich.

MOTHER BELL IS NOT ALONE

But these problems have been surmounted time and again, so that the earnings-dividend experience of telephone company shareholders has been very good. Rising earnings have generated six dividend increases in the past ten years for stockholders of Mother Bell. Some of the smaller so-called independent companies have done even better. Rochester Telephone, for example, increased dividends 14 times in a dozen years. There are a number of other independent telephone companies well worth your consideration, such as the following:

	EARNINGS PER SHARE		Dec. 1975	P/E	1975 Divi-	
	1975	1974	Price	Ratio	dend	Yield
Central Telephone & Utilities	$2.25	$2.11	21	9	$1.20	5.7%
Continental Telephone	1.40	1.53	13	9	1.00	7.7
Mid-Continent Telephone	1.70	1.64	13	8	1.08	8.3
Mountain States Tel. & Tel.	2.24	2.18	20	9	1.52	7.6
New England Tel. & Tel.	2.45	2.58	27	11	2.36	8.7
Pacific Tel. & Tel.	1.76	1.66	15	9	1.20	8.0
Rochester Telephone	1.30	1.33	11	8	.76	6.9
United Telecommunications	1.60	1.62	14	9	1.12	8.0

Like the telephones, electric utilities cannot be excepted, even though they have trouble getting communities to allow them to expand generating facilities—too much pollution of the air with fossil fuel burning plants and thermal pollution in nuclear ones. Nevertheless, industry leaders have great dividend records. American Electric Power, for instance, has boosted the dividend annually for very nearly a generation. Thus, the investor who bought 100 shares of AEP in 1961 for an $85 annual dividend, was getting $170 in 1971, twice as much in just ten years, and now enjoys $200 a year with the virtual certainty that a bit more will be coming in a year or so hence.

Here's another example. We received a routine dividend notice from Cleveland Electric Illuminating the other day. It struck us as a good illustration of why utility stocks have appeal for income year in and year out, even when the stock market fails to behave.

Here are the figures as we received them:

Year	Dividend	Year	Dividend
1958	$0.80	1967	$1.74
1959	0.85	1968	1.89
1960	0.90	1969	2.04
1961	0.95	1970	2.16
1962	1.00	1971	2.24
1963	1.10	1972	2.28
1964	1.20	1973	2.32
1965	1.32	1974	2.40
1966	1.62	1975	2.48*

* Indicated rate.

In a word, the 1958 buyer of Cleveland Electric common has enjoyed a dividend increase every year. His return more than doubled in the first ten years that he held the shares and is now just three times what he started out with.

If he paid the average price for the stock in 1958 (22) today's $2.48 dividend would be a return on that investment of 11%. Even on today's price of 26, the return is a solid 9½%. Longer-term holders have probably done even better, as the notice said that 1975 is the seventy-fourth year of uninterrupted cash dividend payments.

A handful of good electric utility stocks for the income investor in addition to AEP and Cleveland Electric would include stocks such as Atlantic City Electric, Baltimore Gas & Electric, Central Maine Power, Kansas Power & Light, New England Electric System, and Northern States Power.

WATER, WATER EVERYWHERE

One little-known group that offers pretty sure income plus some hope of profit over the long pull is the water utility stocks. Just as certain as death and taxes is our steady uptrend in water consumption. This has been regularly reflected in a similar annual increase in water utility revenues and, in most cases, earnings. Of course, water company profits per share are never likely to explode, but no matter how bad the times, neither are they likely to dry up. Water is just about the last commodity we would forgo. Thus, water company shares have appeal for safety and, at today's prices, high yield.

A fair selection of these would be American Water Works, Elizabethtown Water, Hackensack Water, Indianapolis Water, New Haven Water, Philadelphia Suburban, and Southern California Water.

SOME OTHER DIVIDEND PAYERS

Other industry groups come and go as candidates for an income list. When in disfavor, stocks in a good industrial group can sell to yield nearly twice what they do when they have caught the public favor. Consider the big oils, which used to be a "must" for every portfolio.

Gulf Oil, for example, sold over 40 for much of 1968 and 1969 when the dividend was $1.50. This made for a yield of 3.75%. By 1973 the oils were out of favor, partly because earnings fell and partly because it looked as though the Arabs would take over everything, and the same dividend, still amply covered by earnings, provided a yield of 6½%. General Motors yielded about 5% on a $5.25 dividend in 1965. Eight years later, the yield was 8% on a dividend of the same size.

It's perfectly sane to buy stocks in temporary disfavor for income as long as you can be reasonably certain that the dividend is safe and the company has a good earnings-dividend record. The major oils fit this category. Do not, however, buy a stock for high yield when the earnings-dividend performance is erratic—for that very irregularity may account for the generous return. The market will be telling you in those instances that it "ain't safe."

Other areas worth looking toward for income are in the money business—banks, small loan companies, factors, and those in other forms of "usury." Somehow these moneylenders in the temple always seem to win, and as they do, so do their shareholders.

ON CONSUMING CAPITAL

No discussion of investing in common stocks for income is complete without some comment on the advisability, at times, of spending principal. This seems outright heresy to most of us, but when you study the facts and review the reasoning, it usually proves a good idea.

First, the facts. Common stock yields on average have hovered around 3% a year, or very slightly better, for a decade. The only time they reached 4% or so was for a matter of a few weeks back in the spring of 1970 when the stock market quite literally fell apart, and again, briefly, in the dismal fall of 1974. So for years the average return on common stocks has been skimpy.

Another fact. A sophisticated computer-run project by the University of Chicago has shown that all stocks in a period of 35 years have yielded more than 9% per year compounded, counting both capital appreciation and dividends.

CONVERT SOME GROWTH TO CASH

Then, the reasoning. If your portfolio is paying you 3% in dividends, but really earning you 9% when you take into account capital appreciation, what's wrong with turning some of this growth into cash to supplement the dividend income? Absolutely nothing. Despite the old Yankee rule, "Never spend your principal," it makes perfectly good financial sense to use some of your capital gains as income.

Mutual funds do this regularly. Most pay dividends routinely that are part income and part capital gain. Many also offer withdrawal plans which accomplish the procedure suggested above automatically. So if you want more income, don't be afraid to "eat" some of your stock market profits. You must realize, of course, that there will always be declining markets which will be temporarily upsetting. Again, patience and a long-term perspective will carry you through.

HOW THE FUNDS DO IT

A simple plan for accomplishing this aim is provided by the mutual fund industry. Nearly 300,000 cash withdrawal programs are now in effect with a total value in excess of $5 billion—about 10% of mutual fund assets. Participants receive a realistic income and are able to cope with the problems of inflation.

It's easy to set up one of these systematic withdrawal plans: Just invest $10,000 in a fund with a good record for long-term growth (some funds will start a plan with $5,000). Specify what annual percentage you want to receive, such as 7%, 8%, 9%, or even 10%. The fund will send monthly checks in line with your request. Dividends and capital gains distributions are reinvested and sufficient shares are redeemed (usually at the end of each month) to meet withdrawal requirements.

Some 10-Year Withdrawal Results*

Harbor Fund	$9,923	Mass. Investors Growth	$6,436
Investment Co. of America	9,009	Keystone S-3	6,230
Decatur Income	8,581	National Income Fund	5,987
Putnam Growth	8,501	Keystone S-1	4,812
Security Investment	7,886	Mass. Investors Trust	4,336

* Based on investments of $10,000 with $50 withdrawn each month over ten years 1965–74.

12/31	From Dividends	From Principal	Annual Total	Total Value at Year-End
1965	$374	$226	$600	$10,293
1966	396	204	600	9,038
1967	407	193	600	11,430
1968	483	117	600	13,689
1969	499	101	600	11,282
1970	610	—	610	11,574
1971	621	—	621	12,877
1972	649	—	649	13,039
1973	702	—	702	10,508
1974	734	—	734	8,581

Based on $50 monthly minimum withdrawal and a $10,000 assumed investment on January 1, 1965. Decatur Income Fund is used here as the illustration. This fund has been an above-average performer in the past decade.

The basic idea of the withdrawal concept is illustrated by the 10-year record of a well-known fund as follows. After a decade of regular payments and three down markets, this account was still worth only 15% less than the initial $10,000.

INCOME AND INFLATION

A word here on inflation and income stocks is worthwhile. One of the reasons income stocks return a high yield in inflationary times is the very inflation itself. When inflation intensifies, stocks at first fall, particularly income-type stocks. They fall with the bond market, as lenders say, in effect, if you want my money now you will have to pay me a decent return, plus what those dollars will likely depreciate per year.

A 12% prime rate reflects just this equation, so much for a "real" return and so much to offset inflation. As of this writing, income securities, stocks and bonds, have been through this wringer. Those who thought 5% yields were great a few years ago now happily collect 8%–10%. It wasn't long ago that American Electric Power and a bunch of other growing electric utilities yielded less than 5%. Now they yield closer to 10%.

As interest rates back off, stock prices of such shares will tend to advance and, of course, yields will fall. Thus, with a return to double-digit inflation unlikely, the so-called income stocks seem unusually attractive now for income and profit.

I'D RATHER DO IT MYSELF

Lots of people don't like the idea of mutual funds and would rather run their own investment plans. They can! All they have to do is sell a few shares of their stocks from time to time to supplement dividend income. Here is an example, using a single stock, Exxon, for simplification; other good growth stocks would qualify just as well or better.

Assume approximately $10,000 was invested in Exxon fourteen years ago. This would have given you 200 shares of what was then Standard Oil of New Jersey. You want $75 per month (9%) income from this $10,000 investment, though dividends at first fall considerably short of that sum. The thing to do is to sell enough shares of the stock every year to make up the income shortage, thus:

NUMBER OF SHARES HELD DURING 1962: 200

						AT YEAR'S END	
		Receive	Withdraw			No.	Value of
	Div.	from	from	Annual		Shares	Shares
Year	Rate	Dividends	Capital	Total	Price	Remaining	Remaining
1962	$2.50	$500	$400	$900	59	193	$11,387
1963	2.75	530	370	900	76	188	14,288
1964	3.00	564	336	900	90	184	16,560
1965	3.15	580	320	900	80	180	14,400
1966	3.30	594	306	900	63	176	11,088
1967	3.45	607	293	900	67	172	11,524
1968	3.65	628	272	900	79	169	13,351
1969	3.75	634	266	900	62	165	10,230
1970	3.75	618	282	900	73	161	11,753
1971	3.80	612	288	900	74	157	11,618
1972	3.80	596	304	900	87	154	13,398
1973	5.00	770	130	900	99	152	15,048
1974	5.00	760	140	900	65	150	9,750
1975	5.00	750	150	900	86	148	12,728

So persistent has been the growth of this stock that you would have been able to pay yourself at least 9% annually and still wind up with assets worth more than the original investment in this particular period. This is accomplished despite sale of shares to supplement dividend income.

Of course, the key here is capital gains. The plan works only with stocks that go up. It will not work very well if you try it with slow-moving income issues, such as water stocks discussed earlier in this chapter, but then again they pay so much now, much less capital gain would be required.

So there you are, you can have your cake and eat it too! The underlying philosophy is simply that sound growth stocks will appreciate at least as fast as you trim off this year's growth, thereby keeping your original capital intact. A prudent plan in a good growth fund or individual growth stocks can allow for fairly generous withdrawals while maintaining the value of your initial investment.

8

A Time to Consider Bonds

The next chart shows very clearly what every investor knows—bonds today yield lots more than stocks. As a result, many an investor is putting bonds where his stocks were—in a safety deposit box. But many others don't because bonds are just too unfamiliar. If familiarity breeds contempt, unfamiliarity breeds reluctance.

Bonds didn't use to be so strange to the average investor. In fact, in grandmother's day bonds were the thing for investors. Common stocks were for speculators. However, stocks gained respectability steadily in the late 1930s and 1940s and by the 1950s had thoroughly eclipsed bonds in the average portfolio. Growth was sought after and stocks had it, plus more income, too (see chart p. 80).

BONDS PAY MORE NOW

But in recent years the yield on common stocks has fallen while the interest paid on bonds has risen. American Telephone 8⅞s of 2000, for example, now yield 9% versus nearly 7% on the common.

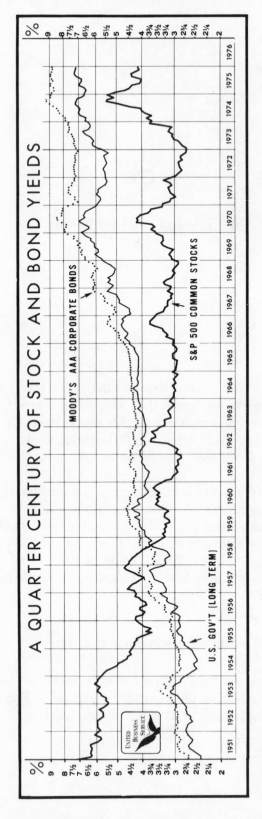

A QUARTER CENTURY OF STOCK AND BOND YIELDS

MOODY'S AAA CORPORATE BONDS

S&P 500 COMMON STOCKS

U.S. GOV'T (LONG TERM)

UNITED BUSINESS SERVICE

%
9
8
7½
7
6½
6
5½
5
4½
4
3¾
3½
3¼
3
2¾
2½
2¼
2

1951 1952 1953 1954 1955 1956 1957 1958 1959 1960 1961 1962 1963 1964 1965 1966 1967 1968 1969 1970 1971 1972 1973 1974 1975 1976

Sources: Moody's Investors Service and Standard & Poor's

Meanwhile, to say that many common shares have failed to grow in recent years is assuredly an understatement. So it is small wonder that investors have been turning increasingly to bonds.

A bond is just a loan to a company or government body at a fixed interest rate (coupon), accompanied by a predetermined expiration date when the loan must be repaid (maturity). Bonds are rated on the risk involved for the holder. Thus, U.S. Treasury issues, backed by the federal government's awesome taxing power, are rated AAA—the very best. Many of our top utility and industrial corporate bonds are rated AAA, too—Exxon and American Telephone, for instance.

As you go down the scale from AAA to A to BB, etc., the risk rises and, in compensation, so does the yield. Generally speaking, most readers buying for income should go no lower than A-rated bonds.

NOTHING IS PERFECT

There are disadvantages to bonds, of course. The most obvious is the lack of growth. Whereas common stocks can increase in value as the U.S. economy expands and the companies they represent prosper, bond values are fixed. Bonds, therefore, are guaranteed not to protect against inflation. Furthermore, bonds can sink in value if yields generally rise. For example, say you purchased a bond yielding 7.5% at "par," or 100 for $1,000 when other bonds were yielding about the same. (Bond prices are quoted on the basis of 100, though the bonds themselves bear face values of $1,000; hence, a bond listed at 96 would cost $960, one listed at 98½ would cost $985, and so on.) Your bond's market value would drop to $940 if bond yields in general rose to 8%. That's because the buyer would want to get an 8% yield, in line with the return he could get elsewhere. Since your bond pays an annual dividend of $75 (7.5% of $1,000), the only way he can realize an 8% return is if he buys the bond for less than $1,000, in this example, $940 (the $75 dividend divided by $940 equals 8%). If interest rates rise to 8.5%, your bond's market value would fall to $880. Conversely, if interest rates fell to 7%, your bond's market value would rise to $1,070. So, when interest rates appear to be headed up, bond buyers should move carefully.

As can be seen in the chart, interest rates on top-quality bonds moved up rather sharply in recent years. However, this upward movement slowed appreciably in mid-1973 and is not likely to carry much further over the foreseeable future. In fact, there are many who believe that 1974 saw the high water mark for bond yields for some time to come. Thus, many bonds rated A or better are attractive investments for the income investor who needs "eating money" now. Following is a representative group for current consideration.

S&P Rating		DECEMBER 1975 Price	Yield
AAA	AT&T 8⅞s, 2000 xw	99	8.8%
A	Central Hudson Gas & Electric 10⅞s, 2005	98	10.8
A	Columbia Gas 10⅛s, 1995	100	10.1
AA	General Motors Acceptance 8s, 1993	92	8.3
A	Maine Yankee Atomic 9.10s, 2002	92	9.1
AA	Pacific Gas & Electric 8s, 2003	85	8.6
A	Philadelphia Electric 11s, 2000	106	10.3
A	Tucson Gas & Electric 10½s, 2005	102	10.3
A	Virginia Electric & Power 10s, 2005	98	10.2
A	Wisconsin Gas 10⅜s, 1995	100	10.6

xw–without warrants.

SOME INVESTORS PREFER MUNICIPALS

In the preceding pages we were discussing straight corporate bonds, not municipals, which we'll cover here and now.

A municipal bond is a loan, too, with the bond certificate representing the promise to pay interest and principal of specific amounts over a specific time span. The only difference between municipals and regular corporate and U.S. Treasury bonds is that they are issued by local governments, with the interest payments *tax-free* for federal income tax purposes.

It is this tax-free status that gives the municipal bond its charm. If a man is in the 40% tax bracket and owns a municipal paying 5.5% in interest, his effective "before-tax" return is 9.17%. As the tax bracket rises, the municipal waxes in appeal. Consider the following table:

If Your Tax Bracket Is:	YOUR EFFECTIVE YIELD FROM THESE COUPONS IS:				
	4.00	4.50	5.00	5.50	6.00
31%	5.80	6.52	7.25	7.97	8.70
40	6.67	7.50	8.33	9.17	10.00
50	8.00	9.00	10.00	11.00	12.00
60	10.00	11.25	12.50	13.75	15.00
70	13.33	15.00	16.67	18.33	20.00

There are dangers and problems in this field, of course, as there are in all other investment areas. First, the municipal, as do all bonds, leaves the holder defenseless against inflation. Second, and more pointedly, the municipal may come from a small town and thus be a correspondingly small issue. In other words, there may be so few of the bonds around that there is no real and ready market. They are, in short, hard to find when you wish to buy, and oftentimes impossible to sell for lack of buyers.

Further, municipal bonds, as all bonds, are sensitive to changes in interest rates. As rates rise, outstanding bonds fall, and vice versa. Thus, since most economists believe that the decline in interest rates since early 1975 has further to go, well-situated municipals are in a good buying range.

Lastly, municipal bonds sell to reflect the credit rating of the issuing community. When New York City's credit rating dropped in 1975, the city's bonds fell promptly in price. So unnerving was this to the financial community that municipal bonds generally sagged in sympathy. However, one of the beauties of municipals and all other bonds at times like these is that bonds held to maturity will always return to par so that you are, in effect, guaranteed your money back.

HOW AND WHAT TO BUY

The way to buy a good municipal is to ask your broker or bank for a decent bond in the amount you have to invest. Most general obligation bonds, backed by the communities' taxing power as they are, are gilt-edged. Many revenue bonds are also of high quality, although here income comes from a specific source, such as bridge or water levies. However, they can become clouded if something threatens their revenue-generating potential—like fuel-shortage-inspired traffic regulations.

One more thing. Municipals of your own state are generally also exempt from state and local taxes. Out-of-your-state municipals will be exempt only from federal taxes. Since there is almost always an adequate supply of good municipals in every state, there is rarely sufficient reason for investors to go out of their own state for tax-exempt investment.

Discussed next are three municipals which are representative of the kind of bonds that would be good purchases for the income-minded, higher-tax-bracket investor today.

Cincinnati, Ohio, 6.50s, 1991. Price: 101 (December 1975). Yield: 6.40%. Cincinnati, oft called the "machine tool capital of the United States," is one of the few prosperous cities in the country. Despite the implications of the nickname, the city enjoys a wide range of industries which produce building materials, chemicals, auto parts, food products, foundry products, jet engines, plastics, and electronics, not to mention soap. Cincinnati is the home of Procter & Gamble. The debt structure is reasonable, and the municipal tax levy is easily adequate to carry this additional indebtedness. Thus, the bonds are rated AA.

Houston, Texas, Water Revenue 6s, 1993. Price: 100 (December 1975). Yield: 6%. These bonds are a first lien on the city's water system. Houston, one of the major industrial complexes of the country, has been a "boom town" since the early days of World War II. The combination of enormous oil wealth and Texan "can do" philosophy which created the city will likely make it even bigger and more prosperous in the future. These bonds are A-rated.

South Windsor, Connecticut, 4.90s, 1990. Price: 82 (December 1975). Yield: 6%. This is a bedroom community outside Hartford, the big eastern insurance center. Most of the housing is single residence, with only two apartment complexes in town. The city is gradually industrializing with major contributions to the local tax collector now being made by Gerber Scientific Instrument, Connecticut Light & Power, J. E. Shepard Company, Gaer Brothers, Kelsey-Ferguson Brick, and Shepard-Pola. Population and property values have moved sharply higher over the past decade. Reflecting the affluent nature of the community, the debt burden is light and these bonds are rated AA.

OTHER AVENUES TO INCOME

There are other good income investments, although many of them probably require above-average sophistication on the part of the investor and certainly demand an above-average level of investable funds.

Yields on three- and six-month Treasury bills got up to 9% at the high in 1974, and even now offer 6%. However, in order to take advantage of this increasingly attractive short-term haven for your funds you have to invest at least $10,000. You can then buy any multiple of $5,000 above that.

The bills are auctioned each Monday. You can place a "non-competitive bid" through your nearest Federal Reserve Bank, either in person or by mail. Your bid will be filled at the average price accepted from competitive bidders. After the three- or six-month period, you will have to cash in the bills or buy new ones at yields existing then.

You can sell them if you need the cash before maturity, but you will lose money if yields are above those when you bought, since the price would have dropped. On the other hand, if yields have dropped, you would get more for the bills.

An important point to remember is that the bills are so-called bearer instruments. That means they're as good as cash, and can be spent by anyone "bearing" them. Therefore, you should be certain to take precaution in obtaining and safeguarding them. For specific instructions about buying such bills and a "tender" (which amounts to an "order blank"), contact your nearest Federal Reserve Bank.

OTHER U.S. OBLIGATIONS

Besides Treasury bills, some other U.S. obligations also currently offer attractive yields with fairly close maturities. One advantage these have over the bills is that some can be obtained in denominations as low as $1,000 and $5,000.

Another plus is that, like bills and other federal obligations, they are exempt from state income taxes. However, they are subject to federal income taxes.

You can buy these bonds through either your stockbroker or your bank. The bank's fee, though, generally is lower than the broker's commission. If you must sell before the bonds or notes mature, you can do it through the bank or broker.

Many of these bonds and notes are currently yielding over 7%. Following are some that might be worthy of your consideration:

	Dec. 1975 Price	Yield to Maturity
U.S. Treasury Notes 6½s, 6-1-77	98.31	7.13%
U.S. Treasury Notes 7⅛s, 5-1-78	99.12	7.35
Federal Land Bank 6.35s, 10-1-77	98.40	7.14
Bank for Co-ops 8s, 10-1-79	100.12	7.84
FIC Bank 7.10s, 1-1-78	99	7.36

SAVINGS ACCOUNTS

Last, but not least, savings banks have been aggressively pushing guaranteed interest accounts or certificates of deposit for savers. Now you can get 7.50% on deposits of four or more years and 7.75% for six years or better in savings institutions, 7.25% and 7.50% respectively in commercial banks. Not bad.

PROFIT IN DISCOUNT BONDS

One other opportunity in bond buying is worth mentioning. It is possible to buy a bond selling at a discount from its maturity price for a sure capital gain when that maturity is reached. Meantime, it will give you a reasonable current, or cash, return.

By way of illustration, suppose you bought the Pacific Telephone 3⅛s of 1981, which sold at 70 during 1973. Your current return on a purchase made at that price would have been 5% in each of the succeeding eight years. Then when the bond matured and was called or refunded you would receive the par value of 100, making a capital gain of 43%.

Obviously, here the trade-off is between income now and income later in the form of a profit. Since the latter, as a capital gain, is taxed at a lower rate than the former, these discount bonds appeal mainly to the lucky soul in a high tax bracket. Of course, this profit is not sudden. The bond will inch up in value from the day you buy it to its maturity date. This means your profit builds steadily and surely and can be taken at any time—with the biggest gain at the end of the line.

HOW DO YOU FIND THEM?

Attractive discount bonds are those A rated or better. They are bonds that were issued by our major corporations some years ago when interest rates were much lower. To compensate for the lower rates at which they were originally sold to investors, these bonds sink in price to the point where they give a current return equal to the going rate. A bond sold to yield 5% several years ago would now sell at 62 so its $50 interest payment would yield 8% plus. Each year toward maturity the discount would narrow slightly until at the end the bond would sell again at "par," or the maturity value, 100.

AND LAST—TIMING IS IMPORTANT

From time to time the Treasury brings out a new issue of bonds or notes that appeals greatly to individual savers. Usually the denomination is reasonable, $1,000 or $5,000, the yield is liberal for the times, and the maturity is short, five years or less. The first of these that I recall were the "magic fives" which came out in the 1950s.

At that time a 5% return on a government obligation seemed outrageously liberal. People lined up in banks, and the offering was a smashing sell-out. More recently, in the fall of 1975, investors plunged $5 billion into some two-year notes yielding 8%-plus. We questioned the wisdom of this rush at the time, reasoning that with inflation close to 7%, an 8.44% return does not look overly generous. Even if the inflation fever subsided to something more like 6% the next year, which seemed likely, the investor would not have been very far ahead. And, as is the case with most fixed-income securities, there is no chance of capital gain in a Treasury note. Of course, with these notes there is no real chance of loss either.

However, compare the possibility of gain or loss and income return on the same money invested for the same period in a Dow-Jones Industrial Average "share." The immediate yield, then about 4.8%, was substantially less, of course. But what about the possibility of gain or loss over the next two years? A Dow "share" was then selling at 10 times earnings. Rarely had it sold much lower in the entire postwar period.

Corporate profits were then recovering from the recession low, and it was easy to anticipate a 25% gain over the coming year. Thus, the probabilities were that if the price-earnings ratio were to hold steady, stock prices would rise about as much as earnings. If so, funds invested in a "share" of the Dow would return through income and capital gains much more than a 8½% Treasury note.

Of course, such arithmetic tends to oversimplify a complex equation. But it does hint at chances for gain or loss facing investors in stocks or bonds. Which you buy depends greatly on when you are buying. In our book, the better chance of winning in inflationary times lies with good common stocks, particularly when they are available at historically low price-earnings ratios.

Of course, if the saver is simply moving money from a savings deposit to a Treasury note, there is no cause for concern. However, if the move is made with what should be stock market money, as it all too often is, the timing is bad, and the saver is the loser.

9

Convertible Securities

Convertible securities, stocks or bonds, are for the profit-oriented investor. Despite current liberal yields, some investors still can't quite shuck the yen for capital gains. For those, the convertible bond or preferred stock is ideal. The fixed dividend or interest coupon provides the income needed, while the knowledge that the issue is convertible into common stock fosters the hope of profit.

Convertibles, both bonds and preferred stocks, tend to be over-looked by most investors most of the time. One important reason, of course, is that many people simply don't understand what they are and how they operate. However, at times when the stock market outlook is a bit hazy and investors begin hurrying into savings banks and high-yielding bond funds, convertibles deserve a close look.

Many provide a satisfactory income return and relatively lim-ited downside risk, but their appeal doesn't stop there. Because they are "swappable" for the company's common shares, they also have capital gain potential.

It works this way. A convertible bond or preferred is a fixed-income security, in that the interest rate or dividend will remain constant. But they possess a special privilege not shared by other bonds and preferreds—they can be exchanged at the holder's option for a specified number of the company's common shares. In effect, then, convertibles provide a long-term call on the common stock. In time, they can be exceedingly profitable.

A "FOR-INSTANCE"

Let's use International Minerals & Chemicals as an example. The company had had its troubles—tremendous overcapacity in one of its principal products, phosphate rock, had brought on ruinous price competition. Earnings collapsed and dividends were omitted. By 1971, the stock had fallen from a 1965 high of nearly 60 to a 1970 low of 8½ and had bounced back to 20. A new management was in, and earnings seemed to have turned the corner. However, worldwide fertilizer demand remained low despite much talk of "imminent famine" in underdeveloped areas, and fertilizer prices remained terribly competitive.

The investor who wanted to bet on the surety that worldwide demand for food would eventually outrun the oversupply of fertilizer (something that finally occurred with a vengeance in 1973) could have bought the stock, a nondividend-paying speculation at 18, or the convertible 4% bond at 58. If he was right on his analysis, he stood to make more on the common, of course, but he would get no income. Meantime, the bond would ease his hunger with a cash return of 6.9%.

By 1974 when food prices had exploded in the United States, the stock had jumped to 45. But the bondholder had done all right, too. His $580 investment in 1971 was now worth $920, a gain of nearly 60%, at much less risk, with two years of income at nearly a 7% level.

PREFERREDS—NEITHER FISH NOR FOWL

We might pause here to describe a regular preferred stock before we mention a convertible preferred. While a bond represents a loan to a company and a common stock a share in the ownership of a company, a preferred stock falls in between, and has some of the advantages and disadvantages of both.

Basically, it simply represents a claim on the earnings of a company after bond interest is paid. Preferred dividends must be paid before the common is even considered for any such distribution. However, if the company goes broke, the preferred, unlike the bond that represents a real creditor, can have no fixed claim on the assets of the business. All its holder gets are the leavings after everyone else is paid off and just before the common stock gets any consideration.

As with a bond, preferred dividends are fixed and, in most cases, cumulative. That is, when earnings fail to cover the preferred dividend and it must be passed or omitted, the company is bound to reinstate the dividend at the regular rate as soon as earnings permit and also make up the omitted payments. However, unlike common share holders, preferred holders have no hope of higher dividends, no matter how prosperous the firm becomes. In short, the bondholders get the assets while the common stockholders get the losses and any earnings gains that develop. The preferred holder just gets his dividends.

For these reasons, preferred stocks do not have a great deal of appeal for most investors. To make them more appealing, and salable, corporations often make them convertible into common. This gives the holder some hope of profit in the future. For example, if a preferred issue were to come out today at $100 with a $8 dividend to yield 8%, it would probably hover right around that price on the open market, depending on changes in interest rates generally.

However, if it were convertible into two shares of common and that common advanced from $40 on the day the preferred was issued to $50 later on, the preferred would likely sell at $110. And every time the common moved up another point from there on it would shove the preferred along ahead of it.

So that's how it works. Following are a few representative convertibles, bonds and preferreds:

	DECEMBER 1975		COMMON STOCK 1975			Conversion Basis (Shares)*	Conversion Value†
	Price	Yield	Price	Dividend	Yield		
Beneficial Corp. $4.30 pfd.	48	9.0%	17	$1.25	7.4	2.10	36
Consolidated Foods $4.50 pfd.	57	8.0	20	1.35	6.8	2.36	47
Travelers Corp. $2.00 pfd.	33	6.0	26	1.08	4.1	1.10	29
Dart Industries $2.00 pfd.	30	6.7	24	.64	2.7	1.00	26
Gulf+Western 5⅛s, 1993	77	7.1	20	.72	3.6	35.50	67
West Point Pepperell 7⅝s, 2000	98	7.9	33	2.00	6.1	26.06	86

* Number of common shares that would be acquired if conversion privilege were exercised.
† Market price of common stock multiplied by number of shares to be obtained in conversion.

WHICH WAY INTEREST RATES?

No discussion of income issues is complete without some comment on the trend of interest rates generally. If interest rates rise significantly, one can expect a prompt and proportionate drop in bond and preferred stock prices for the reasons we explained earlier, and to a lesser extent, in quotations for income-type common stocks.

However, as we said before, we believe that long-term interest rates are about as high as they are likely to go. Thus, bonds are good buys now.

SECTION TWO

Shaping Your Investments
to Tomorrow's World

THE BACK YARD

Most of us have spent the bulk of our adult lives in the incredible affluence of postwar America. Forgotten are the bread lines or "Hoovervilles" of 1933. For the last twenty-five years the wondrous U.S. economic machine has poured a cornucopia over nearly all of us.

We got more and more of everything, and loved it. We went from one- to two- and even three-car families. There was a radio in every room, transistors for the stroller, and color TV's each for parents and the children. Most recently, in a nation which only a generation ago was "one-third ill-housed," we moved into an era of second homes for millions of families.

Not only did we use machines to relieve our drudgeries, but we made them automatic. Let the machines do the laundry or the dishes while "madam" is out. We were also freed of any need to conserve or husband or maintain. It was cheaper to buy anew than repair the old. Our sanitary landfills, incinerators, and garbage scows worked overtime disposing of the old to make room for the new.

That is, until the energy crisis—which showed that our resources were not without limit, that the earth was finite. We shall have to revolutionize our thinking, if not our life-styles. Things will cost too much to throw away. There won't be enough of the new to go around.

For guidelines in this new era we might hark back to these of an earlier America:

> Use it up
> Wear it out
> Make it do
> Or do without

JANUARY 14, 1974

10

Inflation and What to Do About It

Most middle-aged people today—and most investors are middle-aged—cannot ever remember a period of deflation, a time when prices (and wages) generally receded. And that's probably a good thing, for deflation of even a mild nature is painful to most and excruciating to some.

In order to create deflation, the economy would have to be slowed greatly. In short, recessions such as we have seen repeated since World War II have had little impact on the cost of living. The reason that prices have held up so well is that, thanks to full employment, demand has remained strong for all sorts of goods and services. To curtail demand enough to depress prices would require, among other things, an unemployment rate of 12%–15%, or much the worst unemployment we've had in thirty years.

RECIPE FOR REVOLUTION

If federal policy ever did veer in this direction in order to protect the dollar, i.e., preserve its purchasing power by depressing prices, there surely would be enough social unrest to topple the

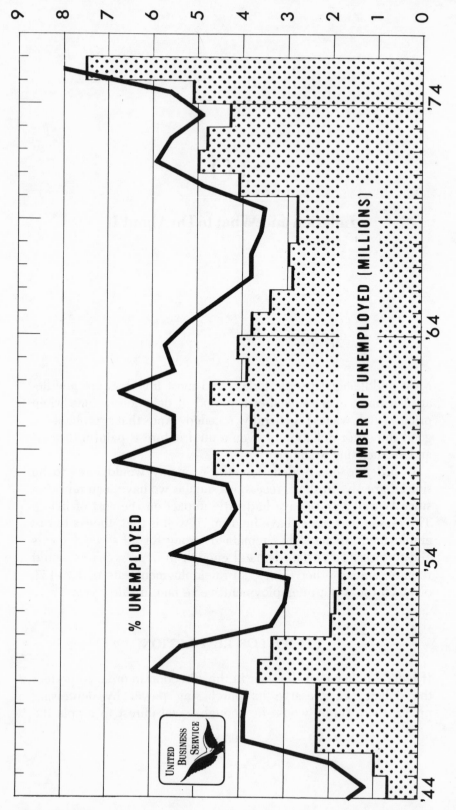

% UNEMPLOYED

NUMBER OF UNEMPLOYED (MILLIONS)

'44   '54   '64   '74

Source: U.S. Department of Labor

party in power. Unemployment of 12%, for example, would mean something like 40% of city dwellers would be out of work and nearly half the nation's teen-agers would likely be jobless.

Clearly, this would be intolerable. Just as clearly, no Administration would tolerate it. A moderate rate of inflation would be infinitely more palatable. Every Administration we've had since World War II—two Republican and three Democratic—has responded similarly. Inflation has been our constant companion all those years. In fact, the worst inflation came with the most conservative Administration.

THE SAVINGS TRAP

We must deduce from all this that inflation is here to stay, the only question being, "How much?" Let's be optimistic and assume a year-in-and-year-out average of 3.5%. What does that do to your savings dollars? It will cut them in half in 20 years, that's what. In other words, the $1,000 you save at age 45 for a pension at 65 will be worth only $500 in real buying power when you actually need it! Of course, savings bank interest will more than offset this at today's rates. Let's suppose that savings banks will pay an average of 5% over this period. Your $1,000 savings will be worth $2,653 and inflation will have reduced that to $1,326 in actual purchasing power.

Another factor to consider here is income taxes. If we apply a 40% tax bracket to this example, we must adjust the savings figure downward from $2,653 to $1,806, then to $903. Thanks to Uncle Sam, then, the saver actually loses by saving! At least if the haven he chooses is in the local savings bank. Of course, if recent inflation rates of 10% or so continue, the pain inflicted on the saver will be infinitely worse.

WHAT HOPE IS THERE?

There are other places to find refuge. Real estate is an obvious one. Many homeowners have enjoyed the inflation protection of their own houses as they have escalated in value over the years. However, few of these homeowners could put their slowly accumulating savings into another house for inflation protection reasons. In the first place, the savings fund is too small, usually. Second, successful investment in real estate often depends a lot on particular neighborhoods, and these have a tendency to change in character with a consequent change in values, up and down.

Even though the upward pace of prices for prime suburban real estate has been breathtaking in recent years, there still are a lot of people holding other types of real estate they wish they didn't. Look in the central cities, and even in some older suburban centers, and see how many of those buildings you would like to own. In some major cities today you can get a "brownstone" for $1 from the city, if you wish. All you have to do is promise to fix it up and live in it for a few years. Is today's shopping center tomorrow's railroad station? Who knows? Therein lies one of the risks in real estate. The real estate line on the next chart reflects all kinds of single-family residences in all sorts of neighborhoods. Thus, it has moved up much more gradually over the years than the bars that mirror mostly the price experience of more desirable single-family suburban residences. These latter are homes that have had FHA mortgage support. However, if you are going to invest in real estate, you would find it very difficult to confine your activities to such prime residences as are indicated by this bar chart. Thus, the dotted line is likely to be more nearly what you would actually experience in long-term investment in real estate.

Rural land values are also notoriously capricious and often vary wildly from one county to the next. Sometimes, it's hard to know what you are really buying. One of our local doctors paid $90,000 not long ago for a 300-acre tract in northeastern Vermont that included a picturesque 90-acre pond. Too late, he found out that the pond is a town water source. Every summer it is drained right down to its muddy bottom, and the state forbids swimming or boating at any time. The poor fellow is now trying to unload the land.

Real estate takes some expertise, therefore, plus management—

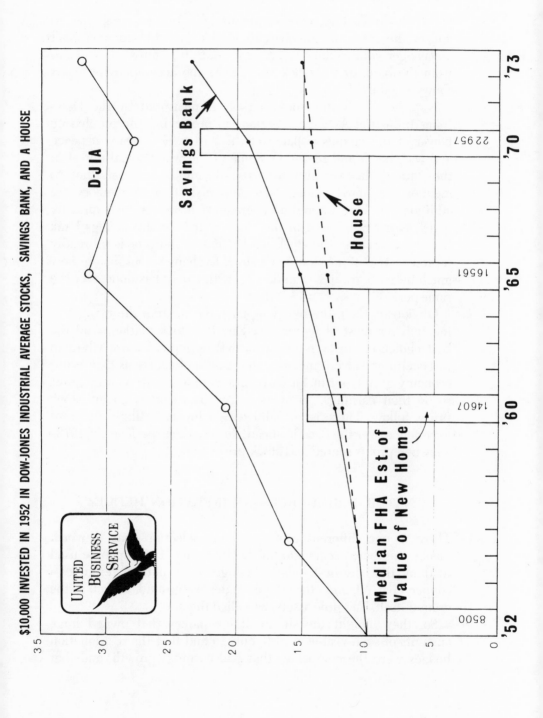

$10,000 INVESTED IN 1952 IN DOW-JONES INDUSTRIAL AVERAGE STOCKS, SAVINGS BANK, AND A HOUSE

D-JIA

Savings Bank

House

Median FHA Est. of
Value of New Home

UNITED
BUSINESS
SERVICE

'52   '60   '65   '70   '73

8500   14607   16561   22957

0   5   10   15   20   25   30   35

buildings won't take care of themselves and someone has to collect the rent—and involves some risk. In addition, you can't always get your savings out of real estate in a hurry, as you can from the bank or the stock market. As the accompanying chart shows, maybe this is a good thing.

Note how well the stock market, as measured by the Dow-Jones Industrial Average, has done in preserving the purchasing power of the savings dollar over the past twenty years of peace and war, boom and recession. Some of the worst social unrest in the nation's history also occurred during those years—not to mention the most beleaguered Administration in memory. In addition, the Dow offered an average 4% income return annually which is not reinvested in the chart as it is in the savings bank line. Furthermore, the stock market line is more or less broadly representative of *all* New York Stock Exchange stocks. Note how much better a group of standard growth stocks has done over the same period.

Obviously, then, the best long-term haven from the ravages of inflation for most of us may well be the stock market. And the best choice of stocks is in the growth group for those who can forgo a bit on current income. The reason, of course, is that as our economy grows, our major corporations follow suit. As they grow, so do their earnings, on average. As the earnings go up, stock prices follow. There is no valid reason for expecting a different experience over the decade ahead, despite the experience of 1973–74, when profits soared and stock prices fell.

NATURAL RESOURCES—AN INFLATION HEDGE?

There is one different route to stock selection that is worth mentioning here. Years ago, in the 1930s and 1940s, people used to think that the best inflation hedges were natural resources—copper, coal, oil, and other things under the ground, as well as the ground itself. Tangible assets, we called them.

So, they bought the shares of companies that owned huge amounts of such visible wealth, only to find that the real inflation hedges were the companies that had earnings growth, and that

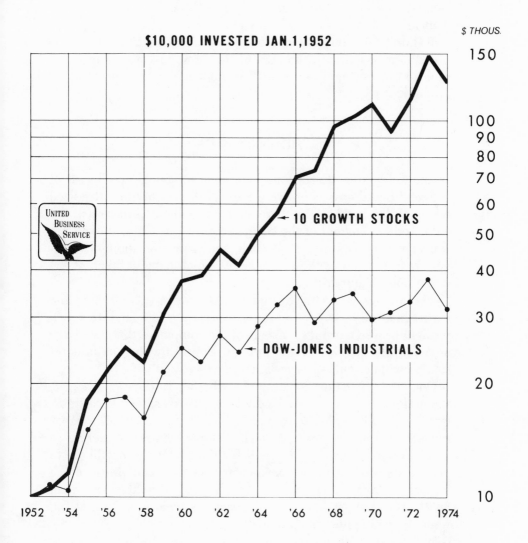

$10,000 INVESTED JAN. 1, 1952

$ THOUS.

150

100
90
80
70

60

50

← 10 GROWTH STOCKS

UNITED
BUSINESS
SERVICE

40

30

DOW-JONES INDUSTRIALS

20

10

1952 '54 '56 '58 '60 '62 '64 '66 '68 '70 '72 1974

tangible assets which didn't produce such growth really didn't matter much to the stock market. IBM and Burroughs with virtually no natural resource assets far outperformed resource-rich Kennecott Copper and St. Joseph Lead (now St. Joe Minerals).

It didn't take long for investors to catch on, and the era of the growth stock began in the 1950s. But now, investors are beginning to wonder again—are there enough natural resources to go around?

DEMAND IS UP

Japan and western Europe are beginning to gobble up all sorts of commodities almost as fast as we are. A thoroughly industrialized Soviet Union is taking its share, and 800 million Chinese will use an incredible amount of the earth's resources as China moves into the twentieth century. Is it time, therefore, for thoughtful investors to reconsider those companies which have so much of the world's physical treasure?

The answer is, well, yes and no. Yes, we are consuming the earth's natural resources at an accelerating rate and this will mean improved earnings for some of the companies that own large amounts of such resources. But no, simply owning natural resources will not guarantee earnings improvement.

One could question, for example, whether International Paper, the nation's largest private landholder, will ever be able to translate its 23-million-plus acres into fast earnings growth. The paper industry just hasn't had that much "oomph." Similarly, there is so much copper around that prices for the metal are not likely to permit big profit gains for Kennecott over the years. Most of the big oil companies are now so entangled in politics—Arabian, South American, European, and Asian, as well as U.S.—that big reserves do not automatically spell big earnings growth.

But there are companies with resources that should produce earnings growth in the years ahead. The shares of some of these will be discussed.

AMAX represents a broadly diversified resource investment. Molybdenum, aluminum, iron ore, coal, and base metals encompass the variety in its holdings. Moreover, since resource- and capital-rich Standard Oil of California has assumed major ownership, AMAX has access to substantial funds to finance its large and ambitious expansion program.

Georgia-Pacific ranks as the king of plywood, as it is the nation's largest producer. Operations, which were altered with the early 1973 spin-off of Louisiana-Pacific, also include significant positions in chemicals and gypsum, and much of its future expansion will occur in these areas. Building products, however, are the chief earnings contributor, accounting for better than 90% of pretax net. The company has 4.5 million acres of reasonably well-situated timberlands.

Masonite Corporation has its principal interest in the production of hardboard, which is enjoying increasingly greater use for building applications. Masonite is the largest hardboard producer, accounting for better than 50% of total domestic output. The long-term record is excellent (better than 14% annual average earnings gains over the past ten years). Masonite holds more than half a million acres in timber reserve and has mineral rights on 170,000 acres, some of which is leased to oil companies.

Mesa Petroleum has had a fine record of oil and gas discoveries and is currently engaged in a stepped-up program of exploration. The company obtained relatively large stakes in the Gulf of Mexico at the 1970, 1972, and 1973 lease sales, all of which were promptly tested. Natural gas is Mesa's main effort with oil secondary but still important. Because of some uncommitted reserves in the Hugoton area and large recent discoveries, the company is able to contract for additional gas sales at rapidly advancing prices. Production growth of both oil and gas has far exceeded the industry's, confirming Mesa's strong reserve position.

Newmont Mining, a holding company, has a substantial stake in copper, gold, lead, silver, uranium, zinc, rhenium, cement, oil, and gas. Copper is most important. In addition to its wholly and partially owned mining operations in the United States, Canada, and South Africa, Newmont has a sizable portfolio of natural resource securities. Income and capital gains from these investments can make a significant contribution to overall profits in some years. Newmont is an attractive long-term investment in the nonferrous field.

Utah International, a worldwide natural resource company, operates mainly in politically stable areas—the United States, Australia, and Canada. Coal is Utah's major single source of revenues and earnings—and about 69% of it is high-quality "metallurgical" coal used in steel making. Copper and uranium each contribute around 13% of sales and iron ore about 5% (but a larger portion of earnings). The long-term record has been outstanding as operations are open pit and the company has not been confronted with the productivity problems that have plagued the deep U.S. mines. Net per share has risen in every year since 1962, averaging over 20% annual growth over the past decade, 1973 registering a sharp gain. With new mines coming on-stream, prices firming, and oil and gas properties acquired, the outlook is favorable.

Weyerhaeuser Company is rich in resources, with high-quality timberlands in the Pacific Northwest totaling some 5.7 million acres. The company is further well positioned with cutting rights on 10.6 million acres in other parts of the globe. Timber continues to be in short supply as world housing demand climbs, reflecting rising living standards. Recently, the U.S. Forest Service has taken steps to upgrade the cut from some national forests, but four or five years may elapse before any noticeable increase in supplies results. Paper lines, about 25% of the total mix, will benefit from new capacity.

BUYING LAND FOR PROFIT

Whatever else it may have taught us, the space program showed us, for sure, that the earth was finite. There are only so much water and so many acres to go around for the 3.7 billion humans who live here now.

Small wonder, then, that land prices have boomed in recent years. U.S. land prices generally have been advancing at an average annual rate of 7%-plus since the late 1950s, choice pieces at a much faster rate. New Hampshire, for example, reports a gain of 20% per year. Hawaiian land values jumped 220% since 1965, and every reader can supply local examples of his own.

Part of the cause is the rise in affluence—more and more Americans can afford a house of their own, and many can now own two. Land is a consumer good. But also the jump in land values can be traced to human heritage. For centuries land was the main source of wealth and security. Those who had it ruled, those who didn't served.

THE TREND IS WORLDWIDE

Land values are rising abroad as well as here, so we are looking at no local phenomenon. Prices have jumped sixfold in Lyons, France, since 1962, while an ordinary house lot around Zurich commands over $100,000. Land is getting scarcer as we humans multiply, and under such conditions prices can go only one way—up.

For those who would like to participate in more than the rising values of "their own little acre," these big landowning companies, in addition to those already covered, have speculative appeal: Burlington Northern, International Paper, Union Camp and Union Pacific.

BUY STOCKS AND HOLD

In summary, the best haven from the inflationary storm is the stock market. There simply are no viable alternatives for most of us. Even so, you must take a long-term view and plan to be patient.

11

Future Shock and the Energy Crisis

Alvin Toffler claims in his book *Future Shock* that times are changing faster and faster, that this change is fueled by a knowledge explosion, which in turn is truly a chain reaction. Thus, men and women who don't face up to this vast acceleration of change will find themselves in the future before they are ready.

Mr. Toffler's claims are hardly an exaggeration. Think of all that has been discovered, invented, produced, and experienced in the brief span of years that you and I have been around. The man of three score and ten courted in a horse and buggy. The man at the half-century mark courted long before penicillin, power steering, or the pill.

And the rate of discovery, invention, and production is accelerating. Today's 25-year-old will see more of this by his fiftieth birthday than we did. What's more, Mr. Toffler says, not only will the physical environment change but so will the cultural, and that is what will be the main threat to the human system.

THE ENERGY CRISIS

Mr. Toffler makes a good case. Certainly we can corroborate his thesis by noting changes in the stock market, which really reflect fundamental social, economic, and political changes. Consider the energy crisis that hit the nation in 1973.

The United States had long experienced an overabundance of energy. Cheap fuel—coal, oil, and natural gas—was one of the principal reasons for our economic dominance over the rest of the world. It reasonably followed, therefore, that the producers of such fuel were excellent long-term investments. For decades, they were.

Oils dominated every professionally run institutional portfolio. Oil companies entered the post–World War II period as giants and continued to grow further and prosper more. They assumed almost the characteristics of sovereign states as they moved through a host of Arab, Asian, and South American nations exploring for and producing oil. Reflecting the steady increase in demand for petroleum products, both here and in Europe, oil earnings seemed in a perpetual uptrend. Dividends grew, too, and oil share prices advanced accordingly. The oils were great for the growth minded.

Then, all of a sudden, the "sovereign states" of Texaco, Exxon, and Gulf seemed to lose their political clout. Overnight they became petitioners rather than dispensers. Earnings continued to rise, all right, but no longer were the major oils in control of their own destinies.

Naturally, oil stock prices fell. The average price-earnings ratio of the group eroded steadily, and yields rose markedly as investors worried about the future. Yesterday's safe and sane investment had abruptly become today's speculation.

Other problems afflicted the industry as well. Pollution through oil spills, sulfurous smoke, and other noxious fumes slowed expansion and pushed up costs. Rare was the city that wanted a new refinery despite the jobs it would create. Thus, shortages developed for which the industry was roundly damned by citizens and government alike.

BUY OR SELL?

So what should investors do today with the oils? Buy them as a sure thing because national demand for oil all but exceeds the available supply, or sell them as political hazards and speculations on a foggy future?

First, one has to separate the international oils from the domestic ones. The latter have it made. Quite obviously, the days of cheap gasoline and heating oil are over. Companies that once competed so fiercely for the available business that profit margins were razor thin now find themselves in a sellers' market. This is truly heaven on earth for domestic companies.

Prices are rushing to higher levels while costs remain under fair control. Except for higher taxes because of the loss of depletion allowances in early 1975, earnings have turned in relatively good performances. Small wonder that leading domestic oil share prices have done well—e.g., Continental Oil, Union Oil, and Atlantic Richfield. There is no reason to expect much worse in the years ahead. Crude prices worldwide are likely to remain relatively high, thanks to the Arabs—thus stimulating the search for more domestic fossil fuels. And, as domestic crude oil prices are decontrolled, companies with good low-cost reserve positions and current exploration and development successes will be the chief beneficiaries.

UNCLE SAM MAY BE COMING

The only risk the domestics really face is government regulation as public utilities. Neither state nor federal governments are likely to take huge "windfall" profits for the industry lying down. This country has never liked cartels, monopolies, or trusts of any kind, and we have sooner or later moved in to bust them up. The idea has always been to let the winds of competition blow fairly on producer and consumer alike.

Thus, the extremely advantageous position of the domestic oils does invite government action of some sort eventually, if not now. This realization will likely keep stock prices in the group at more reasonable price-earnings ratios than would otherwise (or used to be) the case.

THE BIG INTERNATIONALS ARE DIFFERENT

By the big oils, we usually mean those household names with vast interests overseas as well as at home—Gulf, Exxon, Standard of California, and Texaco, as well as a number of pretty large lesser lights. For this group, things are much different. While the domestic part of their operations should bloom as much as anyone's, the international parts are in trouble.

One would argue that the international oil industry is no longer an oil business, but more of a service intermediary, chiefly with marketing responsibilities. Producing-country governments have taken control of production and pricing. However, the international oils still have an important job to do, and diversification efforts may ultimately achieve the most notable success.

TAX COLLECTORS ONLY?

It would not be entirely wrong to say that the big oils were well on their way to becoming simple tax collectors for desert sheikdoms. If so, there is little wonder at the depths to which their share prices have fallen. Meantime, they too are enjoying record profits. Will this continue? It depends not only on our government but on all the governments in those backward, unstable little countries where the oil is produced.

Should the big oils be sold? Our feeling is, yes, someday—but not now. Gulf, in the low 20s, selling at an incredibly low six times earnings and yielding nearly 8% on a dividend covered more than twice over by earnings, is simply too low to sell. But some time next year or the year after at twice the price? Who knows?

HOW ABOUT COAL?

Back in the heyday of John L. Lewis, everyone—except John and the miners, of course—wanted to cut the importance of coal to the economy. Coal was dirty, bulky, and unsightly. Further, John L. could shut off the supply at a moment's notice and did so with frequency, completely untouched by the handwringing of mine-owners, not to mention the rest of us. So the nation cheered as electric utilities turned to oil and applauded the rails as diesels replaced the old steamers. John L. Lewis and his United Mine Workers went into a steady decline as they were less and less able to bring the nation to its knees, and nobody bought coal stocks. Oil was the thing.

COAL COMES BACK

Once again, the future got here before we were ready. Before we knew it, such coals as Eastern Gas & Fuel had gone up almost tenfold while the oils chugged along with the market. From 1961 to 1971 Eastern Gas & Fuel rose from 4½ to 48, while Gulf moved from 18 to 34.

Happily, coal is plentiful. They say at today's consumption rate we have a 300-year supply. It represents 88% of our fuel reserves but amounts to only 20% of our fuel consumption. Unfortunately, much of it is high in sulfur, and with removal as yet either not perfected or too costly, major utilities are under pressure to shift to low-sulfur fuel oil. Similarly, strip miners must restore their lands to meet ecological demands. However, companies with low-sulfur coal and not dependent on strip mining are well situated. By about 1980, western coal reserves, largely undeveloped, probably will be used mainly to generate synthetic gas.

The late 1971 miners' strike, shortages of skilled men, and new safety and health standards reduced output and profits in the early 1970s, but now the outlook is for a steady level of high earnings for the red-hot next decade. Here are two interesting coal stocks.

Eastern Gas & Fuel produces virtually no high-sulfur coal. About
half its output is high-quality metallurgical. It uses few strip
operations. Barge profits are rising sharply, and coal output
should show big gains in coming years.

Westmoreland Coal depends on strip mining for only about 15% of
output, and 95% of the total contains less than 1% sulfur.
Eventually, merger with Penn Virginia (which owns 31% of
the stock) is likely, making possible Big Board listing.

	1974 Revenues (*millions*)	EARNINGS PER SHARE 1975	1974	*Price* Range 1974–75	*Dec.* 1975 Price	*P/E* Ratio	*1975* Divi- dend
Eastern Gas & Fuel	$543.4	$4.00	$3.15	34–8	22	6	$0.80
Westmoreland Coal	399.0	8.69	5.30	56–12	39	4	1.00

WHITHER NATURAL GAS?

Natural gas is another industry that changed its spots when no
one was looking. For years, most of the 1950s and 1960s, in fact,
natural gas was great—it was cheapest to transport, easiest to
burn, and by far cleaner than any other form of fuel. What's
more, much of it was produced and consumed in the same state,
which meant freedom from the strictures of such limiting re-
minders of the federal establishment as the Federal Power Commission. Thus, natural gas stocks were the thing for long-term
growth.

Trouble was, we didn't see the energy crunch coming. Suddenly there were more gas users than the producers could accommodate. The very freedom from the FPC that had encouraged
intrastate production and sales created a high price structure that
made it prohibitive for producers to sell out of state. Those who
did sell out of state—at regulated prices—could not afford to
mount the necessary exploration efforts to find new reserves.
Presto, a serious and growing supply shortage. Natural gas stocks
became "dogs."

For most of the 1960s, Panhandle Eastern Pipeline, one of the major interstate producing and pipeline companies, sold around 35, sometimes more, often less. Although earnings and dividends continued moving upward, making the stock ever cheaper and much more appealing for income, the price of the shares moved little. If there was a limit to the supply of gas available, the long-term growth potential was limited. Until the authorities loosened up, the natural gas stocks, Panhandle included, were not growth issues. (Straw in the wind—Panhandle Eastern announced its intention late in 1973 to build a $400 million coal gasification plant in Wyoming that would produce 90 billion cubic feet of pipeline quality gas per year.)

WHAT NOW?

By 1973, the problems were obvious for gas—too many consumers, too few producers. The Administration, legislators, and regulators began coming to grips with the full implication of the diminishing 11-year supply of gas. Price incentives were offered to producers, liquefied natural gas (LNG) and synthetic natural gas (SNG) were increasingly considered in planning for the future, and selective rationing or allocation of short supplies was planned for some industrial customers. The best-situated stocks perked up, including these representative issues:

Mesa Petroleum, discussed in some detail earlier, has great appeal for someone looking for a stake in natural gas.

Pacific Petroleums is a major Canadian oil and gas producer, and a prime supplier to U.S. pipelines. Exploration is proceeding in several areas. The Canadian government may curb some natural resource exports. However, Canada's estimated gas reserves are far more plentiful than ours. Longer-term plans include the extraction of oil from tar sands.

Southern Natural Resources derives about 60% of net income from wholesaling Louisiana and Texas gas in six southern states. Contract drilling by its 86%-owned Offshore Company provides another 24% of earnings, while oil and gas production, pulp and paper, etc., account for the rest. Offshore Company's growing fleet of drilling vessels gives it a profitable stake in the global search for new oil and gas supplies. In addition, Southern has invested heavily in finding gas in promising offshore Louisiana locations.

Tenneco is probably the safest way to invest in natural gas because it is also big in other important industrial areas—construction equipment and farm machinery, shipbuilding, chemicals, packaging products, and automotive components. The earnings record is good, and for the next few years, anyway, a 10% compounded growth rate is indicated.

113

	1974 Revenues (millions)	EARNINGS PER SHARE		Price Range 1974–75	Dec. 1975 Price	P/E Ratio	1975 Dividend
		1975	1974				
Mesa Petroleum	$ 52	$1.35	$0.39	44–11	19	14	$0.05
Pacific Petroleums	232	2.50	2.13	35–13	27	11	0.80
Southern Natural Resources	523	6.50	5.82	60–27	48	7	1.65
Tenneco	5,002	4.10	4.08	27–17	26	6	1.76

THERE'S STEAM IN YOUR FUTURE

One can't discuss the fast-blooming changes and opportunities in the fuel field without some comment on the development of energy from huge reservoirs of steam deep under the earth's surface. This is using the inner heat of the planet to keep us warm on the surface.

Such geothermal steam is being developed by Union Oil at The Geysers, California, and piped to Pacific Gas & Electric where it is transformed into power. Since 1967 it has grown 455% to 300,000 kilowatts, with 600,000 kilowatts projected for 1975, sufficient for a city the size of San Francisco. Costs run about 5.3 mills per kilowatt-hour versus 7 mills for fossil fuel power and 8.75 mills for nuclear power. It is predicted that geothermal resources could reach 132,000 megawatts by 1985 versus current U.S. power capacity of 350,000 megawatts.

12

Energy Crisis Winners—And Losers

We talked a great deal about the fuel-producing part of the energy crisis in the preceding chapter. But how about the consuming side? Who are the winners and losers there? As has oft been said, 'tis an ill wind that blows no man good.

Some companies are bound to benefit from a shortage of fuel, even if they're only the sweater, ski sock, and woodstove makers in the land. But even of the big corporations, there are many that should find your discomfort a bonanza. Producers of oil and gas drilling equipment will prosper as the nation hastens toward a self-supporting position in oil and gas production. Drilling activities must boom, both on- and off-shore. This means great things for Halliburton, Hughes Tool, Smith International, and Baker Oil Tool.

CINDERELLA REVISITED

Mass transit, America's number one stepchild, will boom inevitably. Gasoline at a dollar or more per gallon, much more expensive automobiles, lower speed limits, and the like, will drive

| | EARNINGS PER SHARE | | Price Range | Dec. 1975 | P/E | 1975 Divi- | |
	1975	1974	1974–75	Price	Ratio	dend	Yield
Baker Oil Tool	$ 3.25	$1.68	59–23	44	14	$0.42	0.9%
Halliburton	10.25	7.61	194–104	142	14	1.32	0.9
Hughes Tool	3.25	1.97	52–18	40	12	0.40	1.0
Smith Inter- national	3.90	1.85	36–10	27	7	0.36	1.3

people aboard trains, trolleys, buses, and subways. San Francisco's BART and Washington, D.C.'s, new "Metro" are signs of the future. Sprawling auto-oriented cities such as Los Angeles, Denver, and Phoenix will simply have to put in buses. Amtrak will need more railroad equipment. Older subways such as those in Boston and New York will need refurbishing.

Who builds the equipment? Pullman, GE (they bought the old Budd Company's transit facilities), General Signal (controls), Rohr, and ACF Industries. Much beleaguered Litton Industries and Boeing are trying to crack the mass transit field. Who knows but what this might not be their salvation! Existing people haulers —Greyhound, Southern Railway, Southern Pacific, and Burlington Northern—should gain a bit of prosperity.

SPEED KILLS

Meantime, slower highway speeds save lives and fenders, as well as gasoline and tires. Thus, casualty losses will abate. Whenever losses decline, the insurance industry gains. Therefore, prospects for such casualty companies as U.S. Fidelity & Guaranty, Safeco, and St. Paul Companies should thus be improved. Multiline companies, which write health, life, etc., as well as auto insurance, like Aetna, Travelers, and Connecticut General, will benefit also, but to a more modest degree.

Dwindling petroleum supplies mean more nuclear and coal-fired generating equipment. This means business for GE, Westinghouse, and Combustion Engineering. Less auto travel means more time at home to "do it yourself." This should help Stanley Works (hand tools), Black & Decker (tools, too), Lowe's Companies (southeastern U.S. supplier for do-it-yourselfers), Disston (more tools), and Sherwin-Williams (paint).

IF IT ISN'T OIL SHALE . . .

There's more oil around, apparently, which is so mixed up in other materials that it hasn't been economical to process. But now, thanks to soaring crude prices, anything goes. Geologists tell us that U.S. shale oil deposits must hold at least a trillion barrels of oil. That is 23 times the amount of regular crude oil now in our proven reserves.

The industry estimates the cost of production at $6 per barrel. With the domestic market price now $7, the industry is eager to get into the shale oil business. The major problem is ecological. To get the oil one must first pulverize the rock. This process leaves vast amounts of silt which actually occupies more space than did the original rock, since the silt is not as dense.

The secondary problem is political; the U.S. government owns 75% of the shale oil lands. Acreage must be leased by government to industry for development, and such things do not always go without a hitch. Thus, predicting earnings from corporate production in shale oil is impossible. But if anyone does win, it should be Cities Service, Continental Oil, Shell, Standard Oil of Indiana, and Union Oil of California.

. . . IT'S ATHABASCA TAR SANDS

Extracting oil from tar sands presents problems that are a bit tougher to solve than getting it out of shale, if only that the tar sands are in Alberta, and owned by Canada. To make matters worse, the Canadian government is discouraging the export of crude by putting a stiff tax on each barrel. Thus, the world price must rise at least by this amount over the per barrel production figure to keep a tar sand producer solvent. A tough assignment.

Great Canadian Oil Sands, Ltd., is the biggest producer thus far and by the end of 1972 had invested $545 million, produced more than 18 million barrels of oil in 1972, and accumulated a total deficit of $88 million. But with world prices much higher now, tar sand efforts could pay off much more satisfactorily. Principal U.S. avenues to investment in the Athabasca tar sands are Standard Oil of Indiana (which owns Amoco Canada), Exxon (Imperial Oil), Gulf (Gulf of Canada), Shell (Shell Canada), and Cities Service (Canada Cities Service). However, the tar sands investment is a very small part of the overall picture of such giant American companies. On the other hand, tar sands operations are so highly speculative that it is only sensible for most of us to make very small nibbles at this stage of the game.

WHO LOSES?

The losers are pretty obvious. People who need oil will pay more and get less. These include anyone in chemicals, leisure time, and travel, three tremendously broad areas in the economy. In the first group are all kinds of petrochemicals from fertilizer to tires. In the second are leisure home builders and furnishers, and producers of outboard motors, skimobiles, skis, snorkels, *ad infinitum*. If you can't get to the lake or mountain, there are a lot of things you won't need!

Then, of course, there are the poor old airlines. They suffered when oil was plentiful and will now suffer because oil is short. This industry has always seemed to face a heads-I-lose-tails-you-win choice in life. Last, consider the autos. After years of giving an increasing share of domestic auto sales to foreigners because it considered small cars almost "un-American," Detroit thought it was saved when the dollar went down in 1971 and 1972. Sales boomed. Imports faltered. But to prove that it could never identify a loser unassisted, Detroit continued to hammer out big cars. When the oil embargo hit, Detroit's favorite machines were getting eight miles to the gallon of gasoline. The industry is much too big to turn on a dime, so again the imports, although much higher priced now, ran away with the small-car market.

TOO LOW TO ABANDON

By year's end 1973, most "losers" in the common stock catalogue were selling much too low. Price-earnings ratios of 4, 5, and 6 and yields of 8% and 10% indicated that the horse had been stolen. It was much too late to lock the barn door then. All that sensible holders of the airlines, autos, etc., could do was hang on and wait for better days.

They came in 1974 and 1975, slowly for airlines and autos, faster for motels and other leisure-time folk. But in most cases the common shares so depressed in 1973 did very well in the succeeding two years. Here, the market anticipated improvement. GM, for instance, nearly doubled in price in 1975 alone.

All of which illustrates two things. One is that major changes in our industrial environment do bring major changes in stock market evaluations. If you can foresee them, fine. The other is that if you do get caught, it's usually desirable to sit tight and let the ingenuity of American business management bail you out.

13

More on Future Shock

When it comes to fast change and resulting future shock, one must give passing mention to the ever higher and faster surges in the prime rate. Right here our interest in the prime (the rate that banks charge their biggest and best borrowers, e.g., American Telephone) is in its rapidity of change rather than its meaning to the nation's credit structure.

The prime rate used to move rather sedately between 2% and 4% in steps of a quarter of a percentage point at a time. For example, it changed only once in 1947, 1948, and 1950, and not at all in 1949. There was only one change in 1957, three in 1958, and two in 1959, when it finally got up to 5%. Now look. There were eleven changes in 1971, eighteen in 1973 when the rate reached 10%—and seventeen in the first half of 1974 when it surged to a record-shattering 12%. Then in the next eighteen months the prime tumbled back to 7%. All this shows is that the tempo of life everywhere, even in the moneylenders' temple, is accelerating.

FOOD: FEAST OR FAMINE

There's hardly an investor around today who doesn't remember the "farm problem." It all started in 1940 or so when the United

States conceived itself to be the breadbasket of the free world. Farmers were encouraged to plant and produce as much as they could on every available acre. When so entreated by the Roosevelt Administration, farmers expressed some fears, based on bitter past experience, of eventual surpluses, ruinous prices, and a return to the poverty of the 1920s and 1930s.

So the federal government came up with a scheme that would support prices with government crop loans. Farmers could borrow against their crops and then on the settlement date pay off the loan, in effect, with dollars or produce. Farm product prices plummeted after the war as the farmers' worst fears were realized. Loans were paid off in product, and government surpluses soared.

Federal subsidies paid to farmers were huge all through the 1950s and well into the 1960s. It was a national disgrace which both political parties blamed on fate and promised to eradicate, as wheat, corn, cotton, and other commodities piled into ever larger surpluses—all at the expense of the hapless taxpayer.

WHO NEEDS A TRACTOR?

Naturally, farm equipment suppliers had an on-again-off-again existence. Things would look up for a few years and then down for a few. Progress, as far as stockholders were concerned, was nonexistent. For example, the farm machines group charted by Securities Research Corporation, which includes Deere, International Harvester, and Massey Ferguson, rose from an index figure of 27 in 1962 to 65 in 1966 and then to 27 again in 1970 and back nearly to 65 in 1972.

THE GREAT GRAIN ROBBERY

Then came the great Soviet wheat caper in 1972 which sparked a boom in food prices the likes of which the world has rarely, if ever, seen. Showing themselves to be real capitalists under their Marxist skins, the Russians came to the United States and on the q.t. bought up all our surplus wheat, and then some. The Russians

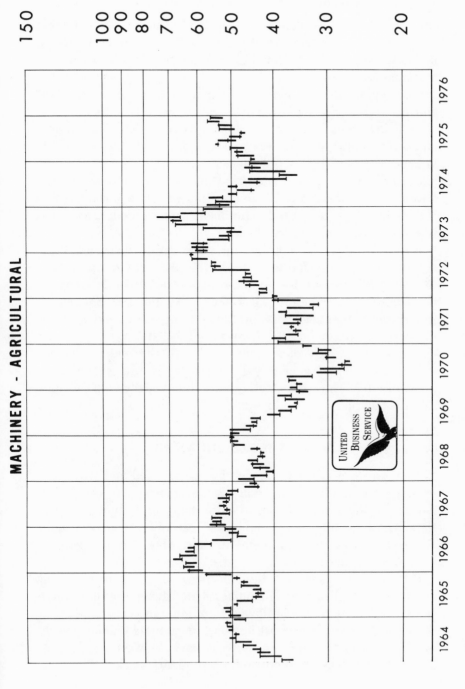

MACHINERY - AGRICULTURAL

150

100
90
80
70
60
50
40

30

20

1964 1965 1966 1967 1968 1969 1970 1971 1972 1973 1974 1975 1976

UNITED
BUSINESS
SERVICE

Data source: Standard & Poor's. Used by permission.

were reacting to an increasing worldwide shortage of food that stemmed from a growing ability of non-western nations to pay for it. Thus, the shortage reflected an increase in demand rather than a decrease in supply.

Once again, U.S. farmers were exhorted to produce, produce, and produce again. Land banks, planting permits, subsidies, and crop loans went out the window as the federal government jammed its multitudinous feet on the production accelerator. Big volume at record prices put the nation's farmers on easy street, and the farm equipment makers went right in after them. You had to know someone to be able to buy new farm machinery in the early 1970s, and used equipment commanded prices that would make an Arab trader blush.

Naturally, this was not lost on some astute investors. Farm equipment stocks began to move, with Deere in particular making new highs during the desultory market of 1973. Here again, the future arrived before we knew it. All the talk by demographers and other scientists, by the Club of Rome, and by other thinkers at Massachusetts Institute of Technology about the growing inevitability of a major famine in the underdeveloped world was ignored generally by those of us who should have known better. Thus, the stock market didn't really come to until the Russians had come and gone.

WATCH WHAT YOU'VE GOT

Author Toffler was right. Change has accelerated and will speed up even more. The future will always come a day early. This means investors will have to do more than simply buy and hold, they'll have to buy, hold, and watch carefully what they hold. Remember those who thought United Shoe irreplaceable or United Fruit unbeatable?

It took the Pennsylvania Railroad decades to lose its blue-chip sheen. United Fruit and United Shoe Machinery lost theirs slowly, too. National Lead moved into limbo in years rather than decades and Scott Paper lost its polish even more quickly. As the world spins faster and faster, we'll have to work harder and harder to stay where we are—with top-quality stocks.

14

ZPG and You

There has been much talk of ZPG—zero population growth—in recent years. It all started with the rather vague worries of a few scientists a couple of decades ago. How long, they wondered, can the earth's population increase before the basic food supply becomes inadequate? How long, was the naturally succeeding question, will the earth's resources permit continued annual economic growth? Does ZPG mean ZEG—zero economic growth—as well?

The first formal warning came from the so-called Club of Rome about ten years ago. This was simply a group of scientists who met in the Eternal City to consider the problem of unlimited population growth. Perhaps more definitive, and certainly more recent, was the publication of *The Limits to Growth* in early 1972 by a group of scientists at the Massachusetts Institute of Technology. They put people and things into a computer model and discovered that mushrooming growth of population and production would reach earthly limits in the next century. Once these limits were reached, shortages of food and fiber and unbearable pollution would bring about the collapse of our industrial society, massive famine, and a convulsive decline in the human population.

In 1973, MIT Professor Carroll Wilson said, after taking part in a high-level meeting on world food problems, "We are now looking at some of the outer limits of global 'carrying mass' in food production. It's becoming marginal to feed the present world population. I had not thought of food as the most critical ceiling. But it is clear to me that you couldn't double the [world] population, as is expected by the year 2000, and still feed them."

Of course, the early 1970s saw two severe famines. One in Bangladesh, the other in Africa. Many Westerners have pooh-poohed the Club of Rome and MIT predictions and have comforted themselves by recalling the dire predictions of Thomas Malthus in his *Essay on Population* published in 1803. In it he theorized that populations tended to grow geometrically while food production advanced arithmetically.

The Malthus predictions failed to take account of the vast new food-producing areas that would come under British and European rule in the 1800s. He failed to see what the potato could do for the poor. Brought back from the New World by the Spaniards, the lowly potato grew so well and in such volume on small peasant plots that it could support whole families.

But, argue Malthus's spiritual descendants, the English economist wasn't wrong in his forecasts, just early. After all, they point out with some accuracy, parts of Asia are already there, with population growing faster than food supplies. Late in 1973, Professor Dennis Meadows of Dartmouth College said, "If I had stood up in March 1972 and said that within two years we would see beef on the black market in this country, and retail food prices up 20% or more, and families going cold for lack of heating oil, I'd have got very long odds. But those things have happened, and they will continue happening."

ZPG, ZEG, AND THE STOCK MARKET

Maybe these people are pushing the facts a bit to fit the theory. But there is enough truth in their observations to make any intelligent investor think twice about stocks. If ZPG is coming, can

ZEG be far behind? And if economic growth slows, what happens to the value of common stocks?

There is no doubt that the U.S. birth rate is plummeting rapidly toward ZPG. In 1972, the fertility rate in this country got down very close to the magic figure of 2.11 births per woman of child-bearing age, which would exactly reproduce the existing population after allowance for children who do not survive and women who do not reproduce. By 1975, the figure was 1.8.

This drop represents in part something that Malthus hoped for, restraint. The ZPG movement itself, Women's Lib, the phenomenon of living together without permanent ties, abortion, and better birth control measures are among the causes of the trend. Can you see any of these changes likely of reversal? Probably not. So, one has to conclude that ZPG is popular and on its way.

The consequences of a slower population growth are already being observed in the behavior of the demand for baby products and services. The Gerber Products Company is diversifying into insurance and containers to offset a declining demand for baby food. Johnson & Johnson is attempting to broaden the market for its products to include adults. Levi Strauss & Company, looking ahead to future apparel market changes, has aggressively gone after the middle-aged customer with all sorts of leisure suits.

Hospitals and elementary schools are feeling the effects of declining birth rates. With maternity wards less intensively utilized, medical resources and personnel are being freed to cope with other types of medical demands. The number of children of elementary school age has fallen by two million since 1969, and a sizable surplus of newly trained teachers exists. A smaller baby crop today assuredly means a smaller number of record-album and transistor-radio-buying teenagers tomorrow.

Despite the above-mentioned changes, a declining birth rate does not mean the end of economic growth. Rising per capita incomes are still likely, as well as higher levels of individual consumption. Such a conclusion is dismaying to those environmentalists who seek a zero growth rate for the total output of the economy. But the likelihood of continued economic expansion means that there is no need for others to push the panic button to reaccelerate population growth.

With slower population growth, a redirection of the uses of the economy's total resources is likely. Obviously, fewer resources will be needed to build and staff maternity wings and elementary schools. But more can be devoted to nursing homes for the elderly. Families will need smaller homes, and the station wagon loaded with kids will be seen less often. But bigger markets for condominiums, apartments, and compact cars will develop.

As population growth slows, the median age of the population and of the labor force will rise. The problems of the elderly will ultimately present a greater claim on the nation's output than they do now. The aging of the labor force will bring new industrial relations problems.

Last, it's well to note that the decline in our birth rate is mirrored in the experience of other industrial societies. One can theorize that as the third world industrializes, its birth rates may decline as well.

CHANGING AREAS OF ECONOMIC GROWTH

In conclusion, then, one can assume that there will continue to be industrial growth which will go on being reflected in higher prices for some stocks. Take mass transit, for instance. In our preoccupation with the private auto we have allowed our mass transit facilities to disintegrate. We now see the error of our ways and money is beginning to trickle in that direction.

It seems obvious that this trickle will become a flood as we face heavy air pollution from individual auto commuters, impossibly overcrowded interstate highways and urban parking facilities, and probably the greatest spur of all, gasoline pushing close to a dollar or more a gallon. (Incidentally, at this writing, Roman drivers are paying just over $1.50 per gallon to fuel their Fiats.)

As we mentioned in an earlier chapter, some old-line companies such as Pullman might well get a new lease on life as mass transit comes into its own again. GE has taken over the old Budd Company transit facilities, and would be another beneficiary. Boeing and Rohr have diversified into mass transit, too, in a valiant attempt to lessen their dependence on the uncertain aerospace industry.

MORE MONEY FOR FUN

The leisure-time people mentioned earlier in the book should win big, since smaller families mean a huge jump in per capita income. The $20,000-a-year couple with two children has a per capita income of $5,000, a whopping 50% more than that for the four-child home. The small family also needs less house, less car, and less of everything else to sustain life than its large counterpart. Think, then, what is available to spend on boats, bikes, and bowling.

FIX IT, PAINT IT, AND MAKE IT DO

Other big beneficiaries of slowed population growth are companies catering to the do-it-yourself crowd. They supply the home power drills, lightweight chain saws, and easy-to-clean-up water-base paints that delight the hearts of urban, suburban, and exurban handymen and women. Additional leisure time in which to tackle home improvement projects is reinforced by the increasing cost of paying George to do it. The growth prospects here remain impressive, ZEG or no.

Here are some companies deep in the do-it-yourself field:

Black & Decker is the oldest and largest of the portable power-tool makers—and has shown the most impressive and consistent growth. The company's aim is to double sales every five years, and over the past decade it has actually exceeded its goal. Roughly 60% of sales come from home markets, 20% from professional markets, and 10% from product service. Nearly half of the total was from outside the United States. Net per share has risen in all but one year since 1958. Always active on the new-product front, the company has a new line of 11 double-insulated tools for home markets. It is also placing greater emphasis on cordless items, such as a new shrub trimmer recently brought out, and foresees "whole new generations" of these tools in future years.

Lowe's Companies, with 89 retail stores in the southeastern United States as of late 1973, has made exceptional progress in the past decade. Earnings per share have risen at a 24% annual rate. Some 60%–65% of sales are to professional buyers, such as builders and contractors, with the rest to retail customers. Lumber and building materials are the big items, but the stores also handle appliances, hardware, home entertainment products, and just about anything the do-it-yourselfer could conceivably need. Housing activity obviously has an effect on Lowe's business, but the construction outlook for the southeastern states is bright.

Standard Brands Paint describes its 50-plus discount retail centers as "paint and decorating supermarkets catering to people who work on their own projects." Most of the units are in California, and about 95% of the paint sold is manufactured by the company itself. Besides paint, other sales contributors include floor and wall coverings, hobby products, brushes and rollers, tools, etc. This is perhaps the "purest" of the do-it-yourself beneficiaries, since it caters almost exclusively to that group. Sales and earnings have shown compounded annual growth rates of 16% and 20%, respectively, over the past decade.

Stanley Works derives almost a third of sales (and a little more of earnings) from tools—electric, hand, garden, and pneumatic. It is also a leading producer of builders' hardware such as hinges, cabinets, and doors. This old-line company has paid dividends annually since 1876. Product demand remains high, occasional acquisitions are being made, and steady earnings gains are looked for.

Wickes Corporation is in a number of fields, including mobile homes, recreational vehicles, and furniture warehouses, which can fall into and out of investor favor. The stock has thus been a volatile performer, even by building-industry standards. Earnings, likewise, have been volatile, but some improvement seems likely. One reason has been the continuing good showing of Wickes's more than 250 lumber and building supply centers, which cater largely to the do-it-yourselfer and are the company's leading earnings source.

	EARNINGS PER SHARE		Price Range	Dec. 1975	P/E	1975 Divi-	
	1975	1974	1974–75	Price	Ratio	dend	Yield
Black & Decker	$0.85	$1.10	42–20	22	26	$0.40	1.8%
Lowe's Cos.	1.21	1.71	52–18	45	37	0.14	0.3
Standard Brands Paint	1.70	1.45	50–23	42	25	0.32	0.7
Stanley Works	2.03	2.57	31–12	21	10	1.04	4.9
Wickes Corp.	0.90	1.54	16–7	8	9	1.00	12.5

THERE'LL ALWAYS BE A GROWTH STOCK

There will always be a growth stock, so don't let the hobgoblins of Rome, MIT, or Dartmouth get to you as far as common stock investments are concerned. There will always be fast-growing areas in which to put your savings dollars, where you can see them multiply.

15

Gold, Devaluation, and Your Dollars

For most of our lives we in the United States have assumed a lordly attitude toward the rest of the world. Generally speaking, we could go wherever we wanted, when we wanted, using the English language and the American dollar almost as handily in Manila or Madrid as we did in Muncie.

In addition, we sold our excess steel and radios to the world's "natives" and bought what we wished of their coffee, copra, and copper. Much of the world was dependent on us. If we failed to buy enough from them, their prices fell, and near starvation followed. Even Europe was sufficiently dependent on the U.S. economy to give credence to the statement that "when the United States gets the sniffles, Europe gets pneumonia."

TRADE, NOT AID

Things began to change in the years immediately following World War II. First came the Marshall Plan which funneled U.S. dollars into the rebuilding of European productive facilities.

Second was the "trade, not aid" philosophy developed by the Eisenhower Administration which encouraged our purchase of European and "third world" products as a way of stimulating their economic growth enough to diminish their need for our aid. All of this worked. As we today can attest, Europe and Japan rose from the rubble of war to great economic heights. This made them, for the first time since our own industrial revolution, truly competitive with us.

During these years the dollar was *the* international currency, having replaced the British pound sterling during World War II. Our dollar was pegged to gold at $35 per ounce. Any foreign nation that did not want the dollars earned from sales to us could turn them into gold.

This was no big thing in the beginning, because most of our dollars were immediately spent when earned. It was our goods the world wanted, not our gold. Furthermore, we had nearly all the world's gold nicely buried underground at Fort Knox. So when a few foreign countries sidled up to our gold window with some excess dollars to swap, hardly anyone paid any attention.

VIETNAM HELPED TURN THE TIDE

During the decade or two immediately following World War II we sold, or exported, much more than we bought, or imported, in the world marketplace. This excess of exports over imports we used to finance all the U.S. troops we had stationed in Europe to keep the peace. We also used the excess to finance the building of Caterpillar Tractor plants in Scotland and Burroughs facilities in France. But as the prosperity we had encouraged, and in part financed, waxed, the need for our dollars to buy goods from us waned.

Our so-called trade surplus—the excess of exports over imports—narrowed and would finance less. By the time the Vietnam war had escalated, we were spending more for foreign military actions than the U.S. economy earned in the world market. Our balance-of-payments surplus became a deficit. This meant a growing number of dollars were being held abroad—dollars that foreigners had increasingly no need to spend here for the things we made.

Thus, the move to exchange dollars for gold gained volume steadily. Our gold reserves sank drastically. This began to cause great alarm. First to panic were those with no trust in "paper money." These are people who believe that gold, unlike all other commodities, has an "intrinsic" value. As far as they were concerned, erosion of the U.S. store of gold was fast reducing the value of dollars to mere paper.

Then came the smart money men. These were the financial experts in the big multinational companies who dealt daily in large amounts of pounds, yen, lira, and marks, as well as dollars. If the dollar was losing its international appeal, they reasoned, why shouldn't we keep as much of our working capital in other more popular and stronger currencies? So they swapped dollars. Then came all sorts of speculators, big and little, all trying to "make a buck" (if you will!) selling dollars.

By the summer of 1971, the dollar was in real trouble. The Nixon Administration realized this and did three things. First, it closed the gold window. No longer would our dwindled gold supply be used to repatriate dollars. Second, it unpegged the dollar. From now on, said the White House in effect, gold buyers can pay what they wish for the yellow metal—for the price of gold will have no bearing on the dollar. As part of this, Washington let the dollar float in a free market. The dollar was no longer in a fixed relationship with foreign currencies. The price of both gold and dollar in foreign currencies fluctuated according to the dictates of supply and demand. Third, it slapped controls on domestic wages and prices in a frontal assault on the raging inflation that was plaguing the U.S. economy. This was in part to help U.S. consumers, but also to show Europeans and other skeptics of the dollar that we were facing squarely our inflation and balance-of-payments problems.

Because of this inflation at home and the adverse balance of payments, the dollar had really become overvalued. In part, too, the dollar had started out overvalued after World War II to help our "trade, not aid" policy. An overvalued currency is one that buys more in a foreign country than it does at home. That's why traveling in Europe was such a bargain in those days. It's also why Volkswagens were so inexpensive and popular for U.S. drivers. By 1971 this overvaluation of the dollar had become so obvious that everyone had to recognize it, and did.

FREE AT LAST

Gold leaped immediately from $35 an ounce, the price for nearly four decades, to $42 or so, a gain of 20%. Also jumping up were the West German mark, the yen, and most other free world currencies as the dollar sank closer to a realistic value. It was allowed to fluctuate, to seek its own level, free to move with supply and demand rather than to be artificially adjusted by the high priests of the international monetary world, the central bankers.

Our problems, however, did not dissipate as rapidly as we had hoped. Gold continued to strengthen, albeit erratically, as did the prices of most other Western currencies along with the Japanese yen. The dollar, in short, continued to melt. This did not help the stock market. No one likes to think that his currency is falling. Probably much of the concern is because most investors do not really understand why dollars go up and down in value.

"IT'S THEIR PROBLEM"

Recurring panics occurred, with the most recent big one coming in early 1973. Treasury Secretary George Shultz announced a major easing of wage and price controls, following a big jump in farm and food prices for two months in a row. This immediately rekindled fears in the hearts of European central bankers of more inflation here, and the dollar fell apart. Gold leaped to around $168 an ounce or more, five times the old official $35 price. Wall Street got the jitters, too, but the fears on Wall Street were misplaced. As we wrote then:

Of course, as Treasury Secretary George Shultz said as recently as December, the problem of too many dollars in Europe and Japan is not ours, but theirs. Just because they have sold us so many Toyotas and VWs that they are loaded with dollars is not our concern. They can always use these dollars to buy Chevrolets, General Motors common, or anything else of the like that is available for purchase or investment in this country. Trouble is, they want to have their cake and eat it too. They want to export heavily to the United States without commensurate imports from us, and they want the dollar to stay firm on foreign exchanges. To keep the dollar up they, the foreign nations, must buy billions in the marketplace. What they ideally ought to do, of course, is let the dollar fall where it will, which would make our products more competitive, theirs less, our exports up, theirs down, and the dollar strong again. But this costs jobs and isn't popular. So there they are—between the devil of too many dollars and the deep blue sea of unemployment. Meantime, the stock market sinks nervously.*

U.S. ON THE BARGAIN COUNTER

Sink the market did, although the declining dollar was far from the only reason. For the next few weeks the dollar became truly undervalued—you could buy more in New York of life's needs with dollars than you could with an equivalent amount of marks in Frankfurt or francs in Paris. This was a good thing for us. Detroit sold more cars, West Germany sold fewer. By early 1975, for example, the VW Beetle had advanced in price on the U.S. market to nearly $3,500 versus $3,300 for a close U.S. competitor. (The author's first Beetle cost $1,800 in 1963!)

Our foodstuffs became so inexpensive for foreigners that our surplus sold out overnight, bringing a prosperity to the farmer that he hadn't enjoyed for decades. Our balance of trade soared as exports boomed and our balance-of-payments deficit disappeared. The pleasure was not unalloyed, of course, as the surge in exports was accompanied by a surge in prices.

* *United Business and Investment Report,* February 12, 1973.

GOLD MINING

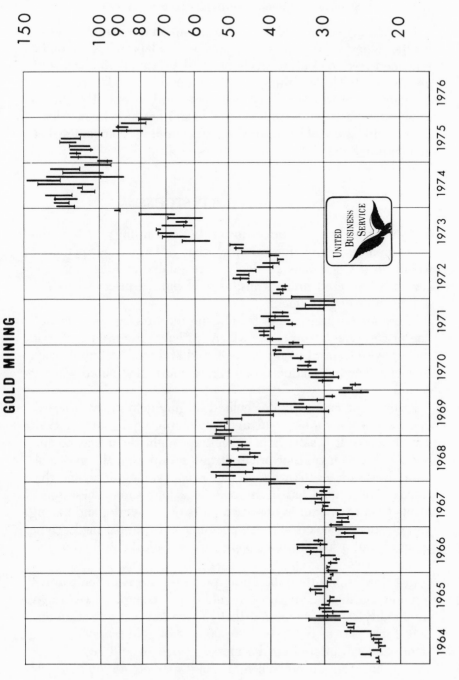

Data source: Standard & Poor's. Used by permission.

Everything we had here really ended up on the bargain counter for foreigners, all because the dollar "collapsed." The dollar remained free to float at levels dictated by supply and demand, clearly the healthiest thing for the economy. Finally, the stock market took heart—or at least began to worry about other things as investors saw that a declining dollar did not hurt them. Meantime, gold stocks—the shares of gold-mining companies—had gone through the roof.

WHICH WAY GOLD STOCKS?

Obviously, higher gold prices meant better earnings for the mining companies. Think, for example, what GM's earnings per share would do if Chevrolets suddenly were salable at four times the currently stickered price! Thus, as gold bullion prices soared, so did the price of gold stocks.

There are several factors behind the recent surge in gold bullion prices. One is monetary, which we have discussed earlier in these pages. Central banks do love gold and tend to buy it when they can. The temptation to sell is rare and easily muted when it occurs.

Perhaps the main stimulus behind surging gold prices is hoarding. People are forever and understandably trying to put their wealth where it is safe. Experience has taught them that no currency holds its own, that prices always go up, that things are almost always better to own than paper money, long term, and that among things, gold has been good for a long time. These sentiments tend to prevail in unsettled parts of the world, and among unsophisticated savers—French peasants and Arabian sheiks come to mind. But a lot of other people, who should know better, feel the same way.

Just how strong these hoarding pressures are is difficult to determine. During the big surge in gold prices a couple of years ago, commodity experts suggested that the market was very thin and that if any part of the 20,000–30,000 tons of gold hoarded on the Continent was offered on the market, prices would collapse. Of course, hoarders do not sell in a rising market. As long as gold prices are rising, they tend to hold on to their "lode," for the very rise in price vindicates their opinion.

Last, industrial demand for gold is growing, largely because the yellow metal is a marvelous conductor, and as such is a well-nigh indispensable ingredient of the super-sophisticated electronic technology of our times.

The performance of gold stocks in recent years is more illustrative of human foibles than it is of the real value of the metal itself. While gold was moving up in price, gold-mining-company shares were flying. In short, investors were betting that if gold bullion could double and double again, it could easily double and double again and again. Lots of people bet on this prospect heavily, not the least notorious of which was a small national bank in Pennsylvania.

This minor fiduciary institution was so sold on gold, and so dubious of the dollar, that it could advertise in the spring of 1974 that it had put most of its trust department funds in gold stocks. The bank looked good then, for gold bullion was selling at a record $180 per ounce, far above the old $35 per ounce official price which had stood for 35 or 40 years. But, while the metal was up fivefold, gold-mining shares were up much more. ASA Ltd., for instance, was selling at 45 or more in the spring of 1974 versus a low around 7 in 1970 and a 3–4 range ten years earlier.

By the end of 1974, bullion prices had inched ahead to $186 per ounce, but the stock market had grown suspicious and gold stocks were on their way down. In 1975, of course, they collapsed as it became ever clearer that the world's central banks were not going back to the gold standard and that gold bullion was nothing more or less than another commodity.

GOLD AS A COMMODITY

If you must speculate in gold, if you feel in your bones that gold will sell for higher and higher prices, just as any scarce commodity (such as oil) will, the way to do it is to buy gold-mining company shares, not gold. Following is a brief description of what we regard as the best four.

| | EARNINGS PER SHARE | | Price Range | Dec. 1975 | P/E | 1975 Divi- |
	1975	1974	1974–75	Price	Ratio	dend
ASA Ltd.	Nil	$37.82	52–26	29	Nil	$0.80
Campbell Red Lake	$1.55	1.76	49–20	19	12	0.82
Dome Mines	3.15	3.59	66–31	31	10	1.10
Homestake Mining	2.75	3.01	70–29	33	12	1.25

ASA Ltd. is a nonleveraged (all common stock capitalization), closed-end investment company which is at least 50% invested in South African gold-mining shares at all times. Remaining investments may be in other South African companies. Because of the concentration in gold mining, the price performance of ASA common follows closely that of the yellow metal.

Campbell Red Lake Mines, Ltd., controlled by Dome Mines, is a leading Canadian gold producer. The 1974 average price received by the mine was roughly $156 per ounce, up from $97.24 in 1973. Operating costs were $29.89 and $26.50 per ounce, respectively, for those years. Its Western Ontario mine is one of the lowest-cost in Canada. Last reported reserves of 1.5 million tons of ore could mean a value of around $210 million at today's market price for gold. This works out to about $26 per share of the outstanding common stock, assuming no more reserves are developed (74,000 tons were added in 1974) and there is no improvement in gold recovery per ton. Given this arithmetic, it is a wonder that proliferating "gold bugs" chased this stock into the upper 40s in 1974. Now near 20, the situation is improved. Again, there is no funded debt ahead of the common, thus no leverage.

Dome Mines, Ltd., is a huge Canadian gold-mining complex with some small interest in oil and gas exploration. Average prices received compare with those of Campbell Red Lake, as do operating costs. There is no debt here, either. Incidentally, some indication of the appeal of gold mining to bankers is the fact that neither of these big Canadian operators has been able to borrow any long-term money!

Homestake Mining Company is the largest and only significant U.S. gold producer. Gold equals 49% of sales. The company also produces lead and zinc (42% of sales), silver (5%), and building materials and uranium (4%). Interestingly enough, even though gold prices spent most of 1974 in the stratosphere, a majority of profits came from lead and zinc, and only 34% from gold. In addition, a small interest in uranium is growing in importance. There is some modest funded debt ahead of the common shares.

THE GLITTERS OF THE KAFFIRS

Not satisfied with risking all on the gold-mining shares listed on the NYSE, which represent mostly Western Hemisphere mines, some brokers, traders, and eternally gullible investors went off after the shares of South African gold producers in 1974.

These are companies working within the Union of South Africa's apartheid social structure. Tense race relations mean even tenser labor management problems. Black miners working in 100-degree temperatures deep underground for white managements in the clean air above ground can become understandably restive. When they do, white government police move in. Eleven protesting miners were shot and killed in 1973. In February 1974, three mines—Free State Geduld, Welkon, and Western Holdings—had 61%, 47%, and 34%, respectively, of their miners walk off the job.

In short, these stocks, called kaffirs (for the native tribes in the area), offer all the risks of Dome and Campbell Red Lake, plus a tinderbox racial situation. In addition, good reliable information on reserves, taxes, and routine operating statistics are very hard to come by. For this reason they are much cheaper in relation to earnings. But cheap or no, our advice is, if you must gamble on gold, use NYSE listed issues.

16

Investing at Home

Sentiment should never be a part of an investment decision. One puts one's dollars where they can earn the most, as long as it is legal. That is obvious. But many of us do let our essential humanity color our investment decisions.

Folks often invest in the companies whose products they like. Many a man owns Caterpillar Tractor because their bright yellow earth-moving machines move him. More than one lady owns Revlon because the products appeal. My own grandmother bought United Fruit back at the turn of the century, much against her banker's advice, because she loved bananas and thought others would too.

THE SOUTHEAST

Lots of people like to invest at home. It's part of their local pride. It's also partly a reflection of the human tendency to distrust a stranger or a strange land, and if you live in Florida or Arizona, the folks in Cleveland are strangers.

This is one human foible that your investment program can tolerate—even prosper on. Consider the southeastern corner of the United States. This has been one of the fastest-growing sections of the country in recent decades, and much more growth is in store. More specifically, look at Florida.

Florida has cast its spell of perpetual sun, sand, and sky over millions of Americans. The dull gray skies of Cleveland, the raw damp winters of Kansas City, and the blustering winds of Chicago have sent a steady stream of Americans south for years. These have not all been elderly retirees, by any means. Many northern emigres to the Sunshine State have been young and vigorous. These people have given Florida a bustling economy and made it a good place to invest.

The population of Florida soared by 37% in the 1960s. The Bureau of the Census is forecasting nine million Floridians by 1980 against seven million today. The economy has grown just as fast, if not faster, for the unemployment rate is well below the national average while personal income is climbing by 10% a year. The state does have its problems, of course. These include our on-again-off-again space program, a growing shortage of water (particularly in the southern part of the state), and urban population densities which those of us in other major metropolitan areas have known well for years.

Here are a half-dozen stocks that offer good growth for the Floridian who wants to keep his money close to home (or to anyone else who doesn't care where his dollars go as long as they grow).

An incidental aside on Disney. Just as I was putting together this chapter, I had a call from a friend bemoaning his recent experience with that stock. "Look at my Disney," he said. "Here it is at 52, down from 120 not much more than a year ago."

He had a point. This represented a drop of nearly 60% in a year when the market as a whole was off only 18% or 19%. However, my friend was looking only at his most recent experience and was thereby ignoring his long-term record in the stock.

He had purchased 25 shares of Disney at 23 back in 1960 for $575. He bought the stock because his kids liked the product and

Six Companies Well-Situated in Florida

Company		Earnings per Share 1975	Earnings per Share 1974	Dec. 1975 Price	P/E Ratio	1975 Dividend	Yield
Disney (Walt)	Major entertainment complex in Florida	$2.00	$1.63	49	25	$0.12	0.2%
Eckerd (Jack)	Operates chain of drugstores and junior department stores	1.32	1.20	26	20	0.36	1.3
Florida Gas	Pipeline supplies Texas and Louisiana gas to Florida	2.40	2.69	14	6	0.90	6.4
Florida Power & Light	Growth utility; serves east coast Florida and Kennedy space center	3.20	2.76	26	8	1.46	5.6
Southeast Banking Corp.	State's largest bank holding company; First National Bank of Miami is largest	1.26	1.79	11	9	0.80	7.2
Winn-Dixie Stores	Large Southern food chain; profits advanced in 29 of past 30 years	2.69	2.52	38	14	1.44	3.7

142

he thought probably others did too. He reasoned that the company very likely had good growth possibilities. He was right, of course.

Over the years the company paid a number of stock dividends, split a couple of times, and offered various rights for additional shares. Because of these, by 1973 my friend had 292 shares. At the price then of 54, those shares were worth $15,768, exactly $15,193 more than his original cost. The profit was an incredible 2500%.

So I advised my friend to take the long view and count his blessings. If one swallow doesn't make a summer, surely one bad year does not wipe out a long-term investment program.

GULF COAST STATES

For those who define home in a bit more liberal terms, the five-state area bordering on the Gulf of Mexico is worth a good look. These states, which include Florida, of course, have enjoyed tremendous growth sparked for the most part by the Defense Department and the space program. Federal spending has greatly stimulated other lines, however, such as electric and gas utilities, housing, transportation (Delta Airlines, for example, which is big in these states and is one of the most solvent of the national air carriers), banking, supermarkets, recreation, and on and on.

In short, the entire area is like Florida—only bigger. Some of the companies participating in this growth that have investment appeal are listed on page 144.

THE SOUTHWEST

Much the same story can be written about the fabled Southwest, from the oil riches of Texas to the zooming economy of Arizona. Any traveler to this area can see the industrial surge of these recently rural landscapes. The smog in once pure Phoenix is a dead giveaway to what's going on. Some stocks to look at in the area are listed on page 145.

Companies Serving Gulf Coast States

Company		EARNINGS PER SHARE 1975	EARNINGS PER SHARE 1974	Dec. 1975 Price	P/E Ratio	1975 Dividend	Yield
First City Bancorporation	Large Houston bank; deposits have risen 25%, profits 30%, since 1959	$3.10	$2.70	23	7	$0.90	3.9%
Gulf States Utilities	Supplies power to growing east Texas and south-central Louisiana	1.70	1.69	14	8	1.12	8.0
Jim Walter Corp.	Semifinished homes; controls Celotex Corp. and a Florida bank	4.05	3.65	34	8	1.00	2.9
Kansas City Southern Industries	Short RR route to Gulf, and connects major cities in Louisiana and Texas	3.50	3.49	16	5	Stock	Nil
Middle South Utilities	Owns Arkansas Power; Louisiana Power; Mississippi Power; New Orleans Public Service	2.05	2.21	15	7	1.26	8.4
Southern Company	Electric holding company; subsidiaries operate in Alabama, Florida, Georgia, Mississippi	1.80	1.41	15	8	1.40	9.3
Southern Natural Resources	Major gas wholesaler in Gulf-Southeast area; has diversified interests	6.50	5.82	48	7	1.65	3.4
Yellow Freight Systems	Important Midwest-Texas trucking routes; also owns freight forwarder	1.65	1.69	34	21	0.40	1.2

144

WELL-ESTABLISHED SOUTHWEST COMPANIES

Company	EARNINGS PER SHARE 1975	1974	Dec. 1975 Price	P/E Ratio	1975 Dividend	Yield
Arizona Public Service — Major supplier of electricity and natural gas in the state	$2.70	$2.34	15	6	$1.36	9.1%
Central & South West — Electric utility holding company	1.80	1.76	16	9	1.16	7.3
First International Bankshares — A Dallas-based multiple-bank holding company	3.50	3.11	40	11	1.10	2.8
Houston Lighting & Power — An electrical utility serving south-central Texas	2.75	2.99	23	8	1.56	6.8
Merchant's Inc. — Over 5,000 miles of trucking routes within Texas	2.90	3.28	14	5	0.80	5.7
Southwestern Life Corp. — A life and group term insurance company	2.55	2.46	25	10	1.00	4.0
Texas Utilities — An electric utility holding company	2.15	2.18	22	10	1.24	5.6
Valley National Bank of Arizona — The largest bank in the Rocky Mountain area	2.10	1.88	16	8	0.81	5.1

CALIFORNIA

No growth story is complete, or even half-done, without mention of the number-one state of the nation—California. Here the superlatives are staggering. The state has more people than any of the other 49. Personal income figures are also tops in the nation.

The Golden State is a major supplier of fruits, vegetables, livestock, chickens, turkeys, and sheep for the country. Despite the rural sound of all this, California is big in mining, manufacturing, and movies. About the only things California lacks are fresh air and fresh water. Its major city, Los Angeles, has about the worst smog in the nation, and attempts to remedy it have produced the toughest auto air pollution control standards in the world.

The water problem is acute—as it is in many other nice places to live—but it is not beyond cure. Better management of existing supplies, plus new sources in the northern part of the state, and maybe even desalinization, should bring along enough water to keep California's amazing growth record intact. We'll bet that when the year 2000 rolls around California is still the number-one state in the nation.

For those who wish to invest here, take a look at the table on the facing page.

THERE'S AN ELECTRIC UTILITY EVERYWHERE

Probably the easiest way to invest at home is in your local electric utility. There's one in every neighborhood and most of them are okay for the investor who likes a good yield combined with slow but sure annual growth.

Some of these utilities have problems, such as huge capital needs for new plant, unfriendly regulatory authorities, special pollution difficulties, or a tough working environment (Con Ed in New York City, for instance). You cannot buy them blind. But again, most of them are okay. The list on page 148 offers a good utility investment for almost every state in the nation.

Five Promising Candidates for California Investment

Company		EARNINGS PER SHARE		Dec. 1975 Price	P/E Ratio	1975 Dividend	Yield
		1975	1974				
BankAmerica Corp.	Giant banking and finance holding company	$4.40	$3.72	42	10	$1.48	3.5%
Pacific Gas & Electric	Large California utility	2.85	3.27	21	7	1.88	9.0
Southern California Edison	Electric utility serving most of southern California outside Los Angeles and San Diego area	3.00	4.10	19	6	1.68	8.8
Standard Brands Paint	Producer and retailer of paints; stores cater to do-it-yourself crowd	1.70	1.45	42	25	0.32	0.7
Times Mirror	Newspaper publisher with interests in forest products, broadcasting, book publishing, and printing	1.35	1.73	19	14	0.50	2.6

State	Company	Dec. 1975 Price	1975 Dividend	Yield
Alabama	Southern Company	15	$1.40	9.3%
Alaska	(No dividend payers here.)	—	—	—
Arizona	Arizona Public Service	15	1.36	9.1
Arkansas	Middle South Utilities	15	1.32	8.8
California	Pacific Gas & Electric	21	1.88	9.0
Colorado	Public Service of Colorado	16	1.20	7.5
Connecticut	Northeast Utilities	10	1.02	10.2
Delaware	Delmarva Power & Light	13	1.20	9.2
Dist. of Columbia	Potomac Electric Power	11	1.16	10.5
Florida	Florida Power & Light	26	1.46	5.6
Georgia	Southern Company	15	1.40	9.3
Hawaii	Hawaiian Electric	22	1.76	8.0
Idaho	Idaho Power	28	2.06	7.4
Illinois	Commonwealth Edison	31	2.30	7.4
Indiana	Public Service of Indiana	40	2.72	6.8
Iowa	Interstate Power	15	1.40	9.3
Kansas	Kansas City Power & Light	26	2.28	8.8
Kentucky	Kentucky Utilities	20	1.80	9.0
Louisiana	Gulf States Utilities	14	1.12	8.0
Maine	Central Maine Power	14	1.34	9.6
Maryland	Baltimore Gas & Electric	23	1.96	8.5
Massachusetts	New England Electric	20	1.78	8.9
Michigan	Consumers Power	19	2.00	10.5
Minnesota	Northern States Power	27	1.84	6.8
Mississippi	Middle South Utilities	15	1.26	8.4
Missouri	Missouri Public Service	10	.84	8.4
Montana	Montana Power	25	1.80	7.2
Nebraska	(Nebraskans use municipal power mostly)	—	—	—
Nevada	Nevada Power	18	1.50	8.3
New Hampshire	Public Service of N.H.	19	1.80	9.5
New Jersey	Atlantic City Electric	18	1.54	8.6
New Mexico	Public Service of New Mexico	19	1.28	6.7
New York	Niagara Mohawk	13	1.24	9.5
North Carolina	Duke Power Company	19	1.40	7.4
North Dakota	Otter Tail Power	17	1.56	9.2
Ohio	Cleveland Electric Illum.	27	2.48	9.2
Oklahoma	Oklahoma Gas & Electric	22	1.40	6.4
Oregon	Pacific Power & Light	21	1.70	8.1
Pennsylvania	Allegheny Power System	19	1.60	8.4
Rhode Island	New England Electric	20	1.78	8.9
South Carolina	South Carolina Electric & Gas	17	1.48	8.7
South Dakota	Otter Tail Power	17	1.56	9.2
Tennessee	(Tennesseans use TVA power mostly)	—	—	—
Texas	Texas Utilities	22	1.24	5.6
Utah	Utah Power & Light	27	2.40	8.9
Vermont	Central Vermont Public Service	11	1.28	11.6
Virginia	Virginia Electric & Power	14	1.18	8.4
Washington	Washington Water Power	19	1.56	8.2
West Virginia	American Electric Power	21	2.00	9.5
Wisconsin	Wisconsin Electric Power	28	1.92	6.9
Wyoming	Black Hills Power & Light	36	2.48	6.9

GAS, NO . . . BANKS, MAYBE

We don't have the same enthusiasm for the gas industry. In the first place, there is not now enough gas to offer the industry much growth potential. In fact, a worsening gas shortage over the years will probably push gas prices up, thereby squeezing gas company earnings between rising costs and lagging rate increases.

But you can get some excellent regional diversification in banks. Although we cannot say that a bank is a bank and one is as good as another, they are really not all that different from one another, either. We might say that one good bank is as good as another good one.

What makes a bank good? Of course, from the investor's point of view, a good bank is one whose earnings grow year after year. This reflects such healthy fundamentals as aggressive loan-making, tight cost control, imaginative management, diversity of operations (consumer credit, international banking, mortgage lending, etc.). But those things are hard for the layman to determine, so he contents himself with the net result—annual earnings.

If profits per share are rising annually, the management must be doing something right. And lots of them are. Here is a good regional list:

Northeast	Citicorp
Mid-Atlantic	First Pennsylvania
Southeast	Southeast Banking
Mid-South	Citizens & Southern
Mid-West	Continental Illinois
Northwest	Seafirst
Far West	Bank America

AND TELEPHONE, TOO

You can even get a little geographical choice in the telephone industry if you look beyond Mother Bell to the infinitely smaller independent companies. Many of these are expanding faster than

Ma Bell, if only because they are starting from a much smaller base. But beyond that, the independent companies tend to serve rural or suburban communities where the growth is faster. So they do have appeal on a fundamental investment basis and one of them may be in your neighborhood. Referring back to the table of telephone companies on page 72, you could make an investment in the following states:

Company	Home State
Central Tel. & Utilities	Nebraska
Continental Telephone	Virginia
Mid-Continent Telephone	Ohio
Mountain States Tel. & Tel.	Colorado
New England Tel. & Tel.	Massachusetts
Pacific Tel. & Tel.	California
Rochester Telephone	New York
United Telecommunications	Kansas

Investing at home, as you can see, can be done. And if the local stocks you buy have equal investment appeal, investing in the neighborhood can make your investment program more fun, too.

17

Mutual Funds—Trap or Panacea?

Mutual funds are simply a new wrapping for an old idea. The idea is to allow an individual to secure some form of professional management plus diversification by putting his money in a common pool with others like himself. He thereby gets something that he would be hard pressed to get on his own.

The idea first flowered mightily in this country in the 1920s. At that time a number of investment trusts were offered to investors. They were closed-end funds in the sense that a fixed number of shares were offered to the public and the proceeds then invested in securities. Thereafter, anyone who wished to participate had to buy the shares from another holder on one of the major exchanges, just as he would General Motors or General Electric.

The experience of these funds was disastrous. They overreached in the famous bull market of the 1920s and collapsed dismally in the even more infamous market of the Great Depression. Obviously, diversification and professional management had not done the stockholders any good at all.

So someone came up with the idea of the mutual fund, organized on a principle similar to that of the mutual insurance industry. The shareholders would own the fund (a lot of good this has done mutual insurance company policy holders!) and could withdraw at any time by simply presenting their shares for redemption. There would be no charge for redemption, only one on the original purchase. In addition, there would be a modest annual management fee which would cover the cost of professional management.

As the idea has thus evolved, then, a share of XYZ mutual fund costs a buyer the net asset value plus a commission. This commission, or "load," is a sales charge generally amounting to 9.3% of the per-share asset value. In each subsequent year, he will pay fund expenses plus a management fee. These usually come to 0.6%–0.7% per share when added together.

For purposes of illustration, say per-share net asset value of XYZ is $10. Our buyer pays that amount, plus the 93-cent load, or $10.93 a share. Suppose the annual charge amounts to 0.7%, or 7 cents a share at $10 net asset value. This charge is made against dividends, so if dividends are set at 4% (or 40 cents a share), the return to the shareholder is 33 cents, or a 3.3% yield.

Mutual funds grew slowly in popularity in the late 1930s and 1940s. However, after World War II interest gained steadily until there were as many as 600 different funds available to the investor by the 1970s. Many of the funds that were brought out in the 1960s were a direct result of the new thinking in investment circles which was called everything but the speculative fever it was.

"Performance" was the watchword during these years. Instead of selling their product as a safe and sane haven for the investor's savings dollar, the mutual fund industry was advertising fast capital gains or, really, rapid riches. Fund competed with fund for asset value gains, first by the year, then by the month.

Tremendous erosion of the dollar in the postwar years left a lot of savers convinced that the stock market was the way to beat inflation. Also, fears of another 1929, long a bugaboo for common stock buyers, seemed less and less likely. Last, people were increasingly convinced that perpetual industrial growth was in the cards for the U.S. economy.

So the blandishments of an army of mutual fund salesmen fell on friendly ears. Common stocks were the thing and mutual funds could get you there, whether you were a big or little investor. Mutual fund managers were not the only ones to be carried away by the new era of "performance" investment management. When McGeorge Bundy left Washington to join the Ford Foundation, he analyzed what was wrong with the management of college endowment funds almost before he located the office water cooler.

PERFORMANCE BY ANY OTHER NAME . . .

Investment policies should be more "aggressive," Mr. Bundy advised. No longer, he implied, should a college endowment fund manager be allowed to buy the blue chips and then sit quietly by. He should be expected to buy the "right" blue chips and then sell them when they were no longer right. He should be buying red chips, too, at least those that were advancing in price. A substantial part of the endowment should be put on the financial frontiers, where the real risk—and reward—was.

Well, this is exactly what the mutual funds did. Portfolio turnover rates soared. Some of the funds actually turned their entire portfolios over two and three times a year. The average quality of holdings plummeted as everyone raced to buy tomorrow's General Motors yesterday.

. . . IS SPECULATION

The ultimate absurdity in the race to beat the other fellow was so-called letter stock—shares of unregistered stock which were bought directly from the issuing company, at a discount from the current market price of already issued shares. However, because they were not registered with the SEC, these shares could not be sold for a considerable period of time, often as much as a year.

In short, so hungry were the performance-minded fund managers that they couldn't wait for shares to be registered, marketed, listed, and seasoned. The result, when the trend of stock prices changed in 1969, was disastrous. Speculative stock prices collapsed, asset values crumbled, and a lot of investors were forever disillusioned with mutual funds. Many a brokerage firm went under, and thousands of salesmen were out on the street.

Redemptions soared after the 1970 market collapse. For the first time since the 1930s, the mutual funds were in trouble. Month after month more people cashed in their shares than bought new ones. In only 4 of the 24 months of 1972 and 1973 did sales match or exceed redemptions. The funds' performance, on average, was poor, too. For example, for the full year 1973 the average fund lost 21% of its value while the Dow-Jones Industrial Average declined only 13%.

The performance of go-go funds was worse. Such funds as Chase (−31%), Davidge (−56%), Edie (−40%), Nicholas Strong (−53%), and New Horizons (−40%) were three and four times worse than the market. This was the reward of letter stock, offbeat speculations in the over-the-counter market, and the unseasoned shares of little-known and virtually embryonic companies in romantic-sounding high technology lines. This was the fruit also of frantic trading and high portfolio turnover.

IN THE DOGHOUSE

By mid-1973, total asset value of mutual funds was $48.1 billion, down 20% from the $57.7 billion reported on June 30, 1972. In the same period, the market was off less than 2%. Mutual funds were truly in the doghouse. But just as investors had been overly enthusiastic about mutual funds in the 1960s, they were overly skeptical of them in the 1970s.

A good all-around mutual fund has plenty to offer. Take Chemical Fund, a broadly diversified fund and one of the industry's best performers, which reported to us in an interview once, "We buy only industry leaders with strong finances, good management, a proven earnings record, and real growth potential." The Chemical Fund portfolio is dominated by stocks rated A by Standard & Poor's. At our last tally, 20% was in drug stocks. Small wonder that Chemical Fund has done well.

A good fund such as Chemical does have something to offer.

First, it gives professional management (not always a plus!) for those who could not otherwise afford it. Second, funds provide the safety inherent in broad diversification for those who can't do it on their own. Third, funds offer convenience—one certificate instead of many, one substantial dividend check instead of a host of small ones, etc.

HOW DO I PICK ONE?

It isn't easy to pick a good mutual fund, but it is possible to pick one to suit your own investment aims. First, look for one with your investment philosophy: Are you a safe and sane type or are you a go-go gambler at heart? Then pick one with a decent record, keeping in mind that this year's superstar may be next year's bomb.

A list of good-quality, growth-minded funds would include these:

LOAD FUNDS

	Assets (millions)	1965–75	Load	Expense Fee	Yield
Broad Street Investing	$ 303	+63	8.5%	0.44%	4.1%
Chemical Fund	829	+118	8.5	0.59	2.4
Fidelity Fund	565	+86	8.5	0.54	4.1
Investment Co. of America	1,178	+116	8.5	0.49	4.7
Keystone S-3	104	+66	8.75	0.64	0.0
Mass. Investors Growth	871	+56	8.5	0.38	1.8
National Investors	638	+89	8.5	0.45	2.5
Pioneer Fund	281	+161	8.5	0.80	3.5
Putnam Investors	426	+107	8.5	0.65	1.8

NO-LOAD FUNDS

In recent years a number of shares have come along that can be bought at asset value with no commission or load. Although the absence of a sales commission alone doesn't make a no-load the thing to buy, such a "discount" does have merit when all else is equal. Following are some attractive no-loads:

NO-LOAD FUNDS

	Assets (millions)	1965–75	Expense Fee	Yield
David L. Babson	$ 179	+90	0.72%	2.7%
deVegh Mutual	77	+62	0.56	3.7
Johnston Mutual	256	+95	0.65	2.2
One William Street	218	+69	0.55	3.0
Price Growth Stock	1,013	+78	0.55	1.3
Scudder Special	83	+65	0.74	2.4

SOMETHING FOR EVERYONE

Whereas funds used to be mostly broadly diversified in common stocks, sufficiently homogenized to suit most everyone, there are now a myriad of specialized funds that have been brought out to meet every conceivable need. In the next chapter we will run through a number of them so you can see what a financial smorgasbord you really face.

We should point out here, however, that these funds have not been created to soothe some inner urge toward generosity on the part of the founders. On the contrary, each fund is created to make money for the founders and managers. To show what a minuscule percentage of assets charged as management fee can mean to the managers, consider these figures from one of Massachusetts' oldest and largest mutual funds. For 1972, the trustees paid themselves, in their capacity as advisers to the fund, a total of $2,951,140. Now admittedly, the adviser does have a few expenses—heat, light, telephone, clerical, research, etc. However, these were not sufficiently pressing to prevent the two top officers (chairman and president) from taking home $518,153 and $322,182, respectively. That very nearly totaled one million dollars for just two men—and this in a bad year for the funds.

The managers of a big New York fund did even better (Gotham is always first). On a $600 million fund they took a management fee of $4.3 million plus $2.3 million in brokerage fees. In other words, they received an amount better than 1% of total fund assets. Again this was in 1972, a difficult year for the industry.

So, the funds are not set up only for the investors' benefit. But neither is General Motors, and we all know that "what's good for General Motors is good for the country." Similarly, a soundly managed fund will do well by the saver's dollar—and by the investment adviser who does the work. The funds have a place in the investment firmament and, very possibly, in your own investment planning.

WHO SHOULD BUY ONE?

It's next to impossible to generalize about who should and who should not buy a mutual fund, but let us try here anyway. First, a person buys a mutual fund in order to obtain professional investment advice. That is the principal reason. If he (or she) is a large enough investor to be able to afford personal investment counsel, he certainly should. Such counsel really is personal. Thus, advice can be specific, tailored to his requirements, goals, etc. For those with sufficient funds to invest, personal counsel fees also may be no more expensive than a mutual fund management fee.

For example, a $300,000 investment counsel account normally involves a fee of 0.5%, or $1,500, which is tax deductible. The same sum invested in Chemical Fund would produce a management fee of 0.59% or $1,770, which is not directly deductible. Some argue that it is, for as it is taken by the fund from your income, it does in turn reduce your tax liability. Anyway, there is no real advantage in seeking professional advice through a mutual fund at this level of investment. Personal counsel offers more for less.

SUPPOSE YOU ARE LITTLE

Going to the other end of the scale, what about the young school-teacher who has a couple of thousand to invest? These are real savings that she won't need tomorrow, barring unforeseen catastrophe. Her salary, her pension fund, her savings, and her insurance are all fixed-income investments. There's no inflation protection there. So she wants something in common stocks. A good mutual fund is a perfect answer.

So is it for the man or woman with $10,000 or $20,000, especially if he or she is not particularly interested in reading annual reports, the *Wall Street Journal* or the pages of some advisory publication. Above this point, the investor should think of going it alone with an advisory service, provided he's interested in doing the work.

Again using Chemical Fund as a "for instance," a $20,000 investment would cost $118. A good published advisory service costs about $100. Obviously, the latter is cheaper, and if you like managing your own funds, better.

LOAD OR NO-LOAD?

If the fund route is the one for you, you do have one more decision to make, load or no-load. Here's how we would approach that question.

First, seek out those funds that seem to have investment aims as close to yours as possible. You will probably find quite a few. Then select those of this group that have the best long-term (five/ten years) records. Then, if there is a no-load fund left after this winnowing process, buy it.

What we are saying, of course, is that price, whether you pay an initial load or commission or not, is secondary to getting a fund with a good record and investment objectives in line with yours.

18

More on Mutual Funds

We painted mutual funds with rather a broad brush in the preceding chapter. We mentioned the difference between the load and no-load funds. In this section we'll discuss some other types of funds which may prove more interesting to some readers.

CLOSED-END FUNDS

While the open-end mutual fund is continually offering new shares to the public and simultaneously redeeming old shares, the closed-end fund issues its shares only once. Thereafter, the buyer of the fund must look to the open market if he wants to "join." He buys Lehman, for example, which is traded on the New York Stock Exchange, just as he buys General Motors: from some other investor who wishes to sell.

Probably the biggest difference between closed-end and open-end funds for most of us is that the closed-end fund often sells at a discount from asset value rather than right at asset value as do the no-load funds, or at a premium over asset value per share as do the load funds.

What's more, the discount tends to widen in a bear market. You get more for your money at the bottom. The premium is larger for a leveraged fund than for one that is not. (A leveraged fund is one whose capital consists partially of preferred stock or debt assets as well as common stock.) Since the premium varies throughout the cycle, this means that while you can always be assured of turning in your open-end fund share at the current net asset value, you never know until the day you sell your closed-end fund shares whether they will go at a discount or premium—and how much of either.

Theoretically, it should be the worst performing funds that show the biggest discounts. Yet there are many good performing closed-ends selling at wide discounts. As the following table indicates, it was only a few years ago that many of these same funds sold at substantial premiums. The situation can very well recur in the future.

Fund	April 1970 Premium*	Dec. 1975 Discount
Adams Express	+1.2%	−23%
Central Securities	+50.0	−37
General American Investors	+0.6	−26
Japan Fund	+22.8	−18
Lehman Corp.	+26.5	−22
Madison	+35.1	−31
Tri-Continental Corp.	+4.8	−22

* Relation between price and per-share asset value.

Otherwise, a broadly diversified closed-end fund is little different from a mutual fund as far as Mr. & Mrs. Average Investor are concerned.

Closed-end companies do very little advertising and don't have a captive sales force to push their shares. Although all closed-ends now have automatic reinvestment plans, only a few offer Keogh and cash-withdrawal plans. Also, stockbrokers are understandably reluctant to recommend them, since the commission involved is considerably less than that obtained from selling a load fund. Like no-loads, closed-end funds aren't "sold"—they have to be "bought."

BALANCED FUNDS

Balanced funds are an old idea, born of the great stock market slide of 1929–32. For those who weren't there, the Dow-Jones Industrials fell from a 1929 high of 386 to a 1932 low of 41. In the process, many an individual stock fell all the way to zero and then disappeared.

Given the magnitude of the disaster, one can easily see why people were somewhat leery of common stock investment in the latter part of the 1930s. To accommodate these fears, balanced funds were brought out. These funds put roughly half of their dollars into bonds and the other half into stocks. The idea was that when stocks retreated in bear markets the bonds would hold firm thereby preserving both income and capital. Then in roaring bull markets stocks would advance, giving the balanced fund holder some of the joys of a rising market.

Theory was one thing, actual practice another. In the long bull market that followed World War II stocks advanced all right, but bonds declined as interest rates rose. Thus, much of the gain provided by stocks was absorbed by bond losses. Naturally, balanced funds lost a lot of their appeal in the process.

In candor, we consider them dull. It's hard to get anywhere in a balanced fund. In fact, investing in a balanced fund is much like canoeing with one foot on the dock. Progress is slight. However, if this sounds like your cup of tea, here are some hoary old-timers in the field: Affiliated Fund, Delaware Fund, Investors Mutual, Massachusetts Investors Trust, Puritan Fund, and Wellington Fund.

BOND FUNDS

A natural sequence in the rise in bond yield, and thus bond popularity, has been the birth of a number of funds concentrating on bonds alone. Seventeen closed-end bond funds came out in 1972 and 1973 as fund managers rushed to capitalize on the boom in bonds.

The appeal of those funds is to the small investor who doesn't really have enough money to diversify in the bond market. The bond funds also offer professional management and convenience —as do stock funds. Most of the bond funds sell at a discount from net asset value per share, and so represent very fair values for the bond buyer.

WHICH WAY INTEREST RATES?

The future of bond fund prices depends, as it does with bonds in general, on the direction of interest rates. If these rise, bond funds will drop, and vice versa. The odds now favor a decline in interest rates from the 1973 peak. Most think this will be slow, and few believe we'll be going back to the 2% Treasury bonds of the 1940s. However, the trend is in the right direction for bond holders. So if bonds are your dish, bond funds may be, too. The list on page 163 gives some good ones.

SUPER-SPECIALIZED FUNDS

There are a few funds that narrow down to some pretty small areas of investment activity. Even so, they shouldn't be totally overlooked by those with a few dollars to save.

There are municipal bond funds that will do for the investor in tax-free bonds what the bond funds discussed earlier in this chapter will do for regular bond buyers. There are convertible bond funds for those who like this route to investment salvation. There are direct-placement funds for the small investor who wants a share of this potentially lucrative field (see page 164).

American General Convertible Securities
Bancroft Convertible
Castle Convertible
E.F. Hutton Tax-Exempt Fund
Municipal Bond Fund
Municipal Investment Trust
Nuveen Tax-Exempt Bond Fund
Putnam Convertible Fund

DECEMBER 1975

Fund Name	Adviser or Sponsor	Assets (millions)	Share Price	% Discount (or premium)*	Indicated Dividend	Indicated Yield
American General Bond	American General Insurance	$200	22	+5.7	$1.98	9.0%
CNA Income Shares	CNA Financial	60	12	−4.5	1.12	9.3
Drexel Bond-Debenture Trading	Drexel Firestone	44	17	−7.1	1.44	8.5
Excelsior Income Shares	U.S. Trust, NY	45	18	−10.03	1.76	9.8
Ft. Dearborn Income Securities	First National Bank of Chicago	100	14	−4.8	1.36	9.7
Hatteras Income Shares	North Carolina National Bank	45	16	−2.6	1.50	9.4
INA Investment Securities	INA Insurance	79	17	−9.1	1.59	9.4
Independence Square Income Secs.	Provident National Bank	29	17	−3.1	1.68	9.9
John Hancock Income Securities	John Hancock Insurance	143	19	−5.1	1.50	7.9
MassMutual Income Investors	Mass. Mutual Life Ins.	125	11	−12.5	1.02	9.3
Montgomery St. Income Securities	Bank of America	171	21	−2.0	1.92	9.0
Mutual of Omaha Interest Shares	Mutual of Omaha Insurance	80	15	+4.1	1.32	8.8
Pacific American Income Shares	United California Bank	79	13	−8.3	1.23	9.5
St. Paul Securities	St. Paul Companies	110	11	−4.4	1.00	9.1
S&P/InterCapital Income Securities	S&P Counseling	168	22	+6.2	1.97	9.0
USLIFE Income Fund	USLIFE Corp.	45	10	+1.3	1.00	10.0

163

* Percentage difference between net asset value and share price.

	In Operation Since	Dec. 1975 Price	Indicated Yield	Approx. % Restricted	Sponsor	Size (million)	Initial Underwriting Price
Federated Income & Private Placement	1972	8	11.3%	11	Federated Investors	$ 36	12
John Hancock Investors	1971	20	9.4	33	John Hancock Life Ins.	115	25
Lincoln Nat'l Direct Placement	1972	17	10.4	36	Lincoln National Life	45	25
MassMutual Corporate Investors	1972	15	10.7	90	Mass. Mutual Life Ins.	74	25
Paul Revere Investors	1971	13	10.2	46	Paul Revere Life Ins.	40	20
Source Capital Common	1968	8	11.9	46	Shareholders Management	155	17½
Source Capital Preferred	1968	23	10.4	—	Shareholders Management	—	—
State Mutual Securities	1973	11	10.0	50	State Mutual Life	91	15

164

Direct-placement funds, a comparatively new concept, really came for the most part out of the big insurance companies that place their own dollars directly. In other words, just as the insurance company lends directly to a major borrower, so will the direct-placement fund. Some of these funds are too new to have a record on which to be judged. However, they are excellently sponsored in that they have good corporate names behind them, and should do well.

MONEY MARKET FUNDS

Proving once again that there is no limit to man's inventiveness when it comes to the pursuit of profit, a brand-new type of fund was born in early 1974. This was the "liquid-asset" fund, designed to take advantage of the high yields available in the short-term money market.

Reflecting inflation and heavy business demand for money, interest rates on such short-term instruments as banks' negotiable certificates of deposit, bankers' acceptances, Treasury bills, other government securities, and prime commercial paper climbed to heretofore unheard of levels of 10%–12%. And these are extremely safe, liquid, and highly stable investments. Among the largest are Dreyfus Liquid Assets and Reserve Fund. These and others are discussed on pages 166 and 167.

LARGE BITES ONLY

Because of this very safety and stability, yields on these short-term investments ran at half this level for most of the post–World War II period. Thus, they had little appeal for the average man. But when rates doubled, they suddenly became major attractions. Trouble is, most of this paper has to be bought in big chunks, way too big for most individuals.

Treasury bills are sold at a $10,000 minimum. Most banks won't go below $25,000 in short-term negotiable certificates of deposit, and only offer a worthwhile rate on amounts of $100,000 or more. So short-term money market investments are hard to come by for the individual investor. Thus, he was effectively shut out of the relatively high yields of 8% or better and restricted to the humdrum 5% to 5.25% available at the corner savings bank.

Now the "money" funds make it easy for the little fellow to prosper with the bigs. One of the first was Reserve Fund, which quickly zoomed to $240 million in assets on the strength of a dividend rate in the 9%–12% range and no decline in asset value in 1973. The investor in one of these funds gets substantially more income than he could ever hope for in a savings bank with an equal level of safety, convenience, and stability.

Most of these new funds are no-load, and most involve a management fee of 0.5% to 1%, plus another 0.25% to 0.5% in expenses. Thus, if short-term rates run around 9%, the money fund buyer at worst should get 7.5% and might get as much as 8.25%. The following are some of the more appealing. Most are relatively new, so do not have extensive past records.

Anchor Reserve Fund has an 8.75% load and is affiliated with the large Anchor group which includes the $621 million Fundamental Investors Fund. Assets approximate $20 million and the fund dates back to the beginning of 1972. The fund's investments are U.S. government and agency securities, as well as commercial paper, CDs, other money market instruments, and corporate bonds maturing within five years. In late 1975 the fund was 75% in commercial paper and 25% in CDs. Yield was running around 7.2%.

Capital Preservation is a $53 million no-load fund which began life as a long-term government bond fund. But about mid-1973 it shifted entirely to U.S. government and agency bonds, all maturing within six months—a position it apparently intends to continue until inflation shows some signs of being curbed. The fund believes that long-term interest rates will continue high and rising while inflation rages. Minimum initial purchases are limited to $1,000; subsequent $10 additions can be made. The fund is independent, managed by its own officers and directors. In late 1975, it was paying a 5.3% annual dividend rate.

Dreyfus Liquid Assets is a member of the Dreyfus family of four mutual funds. Investments are in all types of money market obligations, and virtually all of them mature within two years. Minimum initial investment is $2,500 with subsequent investments of $500 allowed. The fund will attempt to increase yields by active trading. Investments are restricted to government-guaranteed obligations, CDs, and acceptances of banks with at least $1 billion in assets, prime commercial paper or obligations of corporations with at least AA-rated bonds outstanding. A minimum 25% of the assets must consist of obligations issued by banks.

Fund for U.S. Government Securities is in the Federated Securities group but unlike its newer brother, Money Market Management, does not confine its investments to short-term securities. Instead, it aims at flexibility—short-term securities when interest rates are expected to rise, switching to longer maturities when rates fall. In late 1975, the fund was some 47% short- and intermediate-term government securities, the rest long-term paper. Clearly, the fund's ability to forecast interest rate swings is crucial. As the name implies, all investments are U.S. government or agency securities. Minimum investment is $250. Assets approximate $100 million. Dividends are paid monthly and late 1975 yield was around 7%. Load is 1.5% on up to $10,000 invested; 1% up to $25,000. Price stability is high.

Money Market Management is a no-load fund in the Federated Securities group (Boston Foundation, Fund for U.S. Government Securities, Lutheran Brotherhood Funds). Investments are limited to money market instruments maturing in one year or less. The minimum investment is $1,000.

Reserve Fund was one of the first in the field. In late 1975, the fund investments were all CDs or bankers' acceptances of domestic banks with assets above $500 million. Maturities averaged below one month. Minimum investment is $1,000. Reserve is an independent fund (not affiliated) managed by its own officers and directors.

FOREIGN FUNDS

Funds invested in foreign securities performed extremely well in 1973. In fact, when one compares ASA Limited (up 112% for 1973) or International Investors (up 94%) with some of the leading domestic funds, one could wonder if a decimal point had been misplaced. But the truth is, the foreign funds did much, much better than any domestic fund in 1973. There are a number of reasons for this.

BEATING A CHEAPER DOLLAR

First, dollar devaluation had pushed up foreign security values. For example, the West German mark in mid-1973 was selling 25% higher in terms of dollars than it was the year before. This means that any fund invested in West German securities in 1973 would be selling 25% above 1972 levels, just because of the change in currency values. This made foreign funds attractive as a hedge against any further decline in the value of the dollar. Of course, it also means foreign funds suffer as the dollar stages a comeback in international money markets.

Second, leading foreign economies have been growing at literally dizzying rates. Japan, for example, has grown by 15% annually in recent years and actually doubled its GNP from 1966 through 1971. In the same period, our own GNP rose a more modest 40%.

Third, and probably least important, was speculation over the possible demise of the interest equalization tax. Instituted in 1963 by the Kennedy Administration to ease our balance-of-payments problems, this tax was eliminated early in 1974. The levy amounted to a premium added to the price of a foreign security.

GOLD GLITTERS MOST

In recent years, the best performers among foreign mutual funds have been those specialized funds invested primarily in the shares of gold-mining companies. The yellow metal sold at about $65 an ounce in January 1973 and at about $120 a year later. In the period 1970–1974, gold prices soared an incredible 400%, from $34.75 per ounce to $166.50. Small wonder that gold stock prices surged, taking such gold-specializing mutual funds as ASA and International Investors with them.

There are presently five mutual funds investing abroad that are interesting to U.S. investors. Our favorites are Canadian, Scudder, and Japan.

Canadian Fund is a U.S.-operated fund that concentrates exclusively on Canadian securities, with growth of capital its principal investment objective. Present holdings are spread among several different industries with chief emphasis on natural resources. Energy-related stocks make up the largest sector of the portfolio, accounting for more than 20% of assets. Fund performance was up +11% for 1975 and up strongly in early 1976.

Scudder International Fund, a U.S.-based no-load fund, has thirteen countries in its portfolio. Fund holdings consist primarily of what management defines as high-quality stocks selling at lower P/E ratios than those in this country.

Japan Fund is a U.S.-based closed-end fund investing exclusively in Japanese companies. As a direct result of a boom in the Japanese economy, the fund has been a top performer among foreign funds. Most of the companies found in the portfolio are selling at relatively low P/E ratios, and this should provide a cushion against any market downtrend. From a long-term viewpoint, the Japanese economy is still expected to grow faster than those of many other industrialized countries.

ASA Limited (formerly American South African) and *International Investors* are essentially speculations on the further strength in gold prices. With the U.S. balance-of-payments situation improving and the dollar strengthening, we are a bit leery of speculating in this area. Thus, we would "pass" on these two for now.

| | % CHANGE IN NET ASSET VALUE | | | Investment | Size |
	1974	1973	1970–75	Specialty	(mil.)
Canadian Fund	−21	−2	+27	Canada	$ 27
Scudder International	−22	−7	+17	International	17
Japan Fund	−7	−19	+66	Japan	128
ASA Limited	+37	+125	+181	Gold	193
International Investors	+11	+93	+157	Gold	89

REITs MAY PAY GENEROUSLY

One of the newer wrinkles in the fund field is real estate investment trusts—REITs. These funds invest not in securities but in real estate mortgages. For the investor who really distrusts paper money, stock certificates, and the like, for the man or woman who wants money in something tangible, REITs may have appeal as speculation.

REITs raise money in two ways. First, they sell shares to the public, as do all investment funds. Then, they supplement this with borrowing. Some borrow from banks, others offer the public bonds. But either way the debt gives the shares leverage. The profit for a REIT comes from the spread between what it pays for its money and what it gets when it lends it. Just like a bank.

Generally, REIT interest rates are tied to the prime rate (the rate at which the banking industry lends money to its best risks); thus REITs should not suffer as much as they otherwise might by the bobbing and weaving of interest rates over the years. Also, as long as a REIT pays out at least 90% of net earnings as dividends, it is not liable for any federal taxes.

On the negative side, REITs tend to lend on riskier properties and construction projects in their earlier phases, which may or may not come off. Earnings and dividends tend to contract with volume during periods of tight money. Thus, the industry had a tough time in the severe money crunch of 1974. Nevertheless, all things considered, the record for this industry with $13 billion in assets has not been too bad. For those willing to take risks for better than average future income and capital gain, the better REITs are worth considering on a speculative basis.

Here are a representative few of the more than 200 available:

| | EARNINGS PER SHARE | | Price Range | Dec. 1975 | P/E | Divi- | |
	1975	1974	1974–75	Price	Ratio	dend*	Yield
Chase Manhattan	$*d4.07	$2.13	43–2	3	—	nil	—
Equitable Life Mortgage & Realty	1.95	1.92	23–10	18	11	2.04	11.3
Lomas & Nettleton	2.02	3.82	35–12	12	6	2.60	21.7
MONY Mortgage	0.71	0.80	9–4	7	10	0.76	10.9

* Annualization of latest quarterly payment rate as of December 2, 1975. *d* = deficit.

Chase Manhattan Mortgage and Realty, once the industry leader by virtue of its sponsorship, coupled with aggressive lending, has huge non-earning investments which have desperately restricted interest income. The stock at 3 may have discounted these troubles and has appeal as an outright speculation.

Equitable Life Mortage & Realty passed through the "troubles" of the 1975 real estate market better than most REITs because of emphasis on longer-term mortgages, generally of higher quality than those for shorter terms. Non-earning assets remain low, and dividends are not likely to vary much.

Lomas & Nettleton Mortgage Investors is affiliated with the leading mortgage banker, from which it derives its name. The adviser-parent helps originate a constant flow of first mortgage and construction loans.

MONY Mortgage Investors can rely on its adviser—Mutual of New York, one of the nation's most respected insurance companies—for a steady supply of mortgage loans for its expanding portfolio. This REIT plans again to emphasize long-term mortgages, including those with equity features.

A "DO-IT-YOURSELF" MUTUAL FUND

Many investors are reluctant to trust anyone with their own financial affairs. Whatever is done with their savings they want to do themselves. To them a savings bank passbook and a bundle of stock certificates in the safety deposit box are infinitely more attractive than a share of a mutual fund.

They do wonder at times, however, if they really get enough diversification this way. The answer is that the individual investor can get enough diversification nowadays even if his funds are limited. It is possible because so many of our major corporations have been so tremendously diversified on their own since World War II.

Look at General Electric, for example, in the table. This industrial giant makes air conditioners, clothes washers, dryers, dish-

SEVEN COMPANIES—THIRTY INDUSTRIES

Industry	AMF Inc.	Continental Oil	General Elec.	Minn. M. & M.	Northwest Industries	Tenneco Inc.	Warner-Lambert
Aerospace			*	*			
Agricultural Chemicals					*	*	
Atomic Power		*	*	*		*	
Automation	*		*	*			
Automobile Supplies	*	*		*	*	*	
Building Supplies		*	*	*	*		
Chemicals		*	*	*	*	*	*
Coal		*					
Computers			*	*			
Consumer Goods	*		*	*	*		*
Drugs				*			*
Electrical Equipment	*		*	*	*		
Electronics	*		*	*			*
Finance			*			*	
Food & Beverages	*				*	*	*
Household Goods & Clothing	*	*	*	*	*		*
Leisure Time	*		*	*		*	*
Machinery	*		*		*	*	
Medical Supplies			*	*			*
Natural Gas	*	*			*	*	
Office Equipment			*	*			
Oil	*	*			*	*	
Optics				*			*
Packaging				*		*	
Plastics		*	*	*		*	
Publishing				*			
Radio-TV			*	*			
Shipbuilding	*					*	
Textile Products				*	*		
Toiletries & Cosmetics		*					*

washers, lamps, radio and TV receivers, ranges, refrigerators, stereo equipment, and tape recorders for the consumer market.

It also offers batteries, capacitators, computer time-sharing, controls, medical systems, plastics, silicones, etc., etc., to the industrial customer. GE is one of the biggest companies in aircraft jet engines, both military and commercial, and in nuclear power. Through GE Credit Corp., the company is one of the nation's largest finance companies.

Always in step with the future, GE management prepared for the inevitable resurgence of mass transit by buying the car-building facilities of Budd Company. With yearly sales of $10 billion or more, General Electric is almost a one-company mutual fund by itself. Add a few other giants like it to your portfolio and you will have a well-diversified investment program of your own. Here's a sample:

No. of Shares	Dec. 1975 Price	Cost	Dividend	Annual Income
150 AMF Inc.	21	$ 3,150	$1.24	$186
50 Continental Oil	58	2,900	2.00	100
70 General Electric	49	3,430	1.60	112
60 Minnesota Mining & Mfg.	61	3,660	1.35	81
100 Northwest Industries	30	3,000	1.75	175
100 Tenneco Inc.	26	2,600	1.76	176
100 Warner-Lambert	37	3,100	0.92	92
		$21,840		$922

Polishing Your Investment Techniques

THE BACK YARD

We've been telling people for years that the only way to get rich in the stock market is slowly. There is no fast route. We always thought that professional investors agreed with us—that it was the little fellow, the unsophisticated, who tried to do it in a hurry.

We were wrong. We had it backwards, it seems. The little fellow is apparently using his head and buying good stocks for the long pull. It is the big fellow, or the institutional portfolio manager, who is in a hurry—who can't wait for profit tomorrow—who has to have it today.

Out of a group of 25 big name pension funds reporting recently, five turned their portfolios over 50% or more in one year, two bested 86%, and two others passed the 100% mark. One portfolio was turned over almost twice in one year—169%.

To show that big turnover isn't necessarily the road to riches, look at the figures of five no-load mutual funds which were among the top performers for the five years 1968–72.

	Net Asset Value Gain	Portfolio Turnover
David L. Babson	+70%	21.1%
Johnston Mutual	+60	29.0
Pine Street	+45	34.9
Price Growth	+54	20.0
Stein Capital Opport.	+65	29.6

Of course, the day is gone when you can buy a bunch of stocks and lock them away forever, but 50%, 100%, or 150% turnover seems rather extreme, and expensive.

MARCH 26, 1973

19

Making Money in Stocks

In the last analysis, people buy stocks to make money. We call it different things. We say we are investing in Mobil or we're putting something aside in General Motors, but really we are trying to make our money make more money. We have suggested earlier in this book that the best way to do this is to buy good stocks and hold them. But you might wonder if there is not a faster and perhaps more sure road to riches. Shouldn't you sell stocks when they get "high" and buy them back when they get "low"?

Everyone can see the cycles in stock prices. Look at any chart. Why not take advantage of these swings? This reminds us of some correspondence we had back in 1973 with one of our clients who wrote in to express his dismay over the course of the stock market—not to mention his stocks—in recent months. A glance at the big chart in the front of the book will show painfully the course of prices which prompted his letter, which follows, and the substance of our reply.

Dear Mr. Sargent,
I've long wanted to point out to you what I think is the principal weakness of your service. It is your inability to

anticipate a bear market. As the market advances you should
tell your subscribers to sell, gradually, so that when the top
is inevitably reached, they will have a sizable amount of cash
to be reinvested later on, lower down. . . .

It sounds good, we replied to our correspondent. But it is much
easier said than done. If an adviser could call market turns with
this sort of accuracy, his people would soon acquire ownership of
everything on this tired old world and shortly thereafter have a
first mortgage on the moon.

Sometimes, of course, one can take advantage of high points in
the market. Back in 1961, when the Dow-Jones Industrial Average was selling at 22 times earnings, it did not take genius to
reason that the market was vulnerable. Neither did it, really, in
1968, when speculation over-the-counter and on the American
Stock Exchange was furious and obvious.

TOPS ARE HARD TO FIND

But things weren't so obvious in 1966, nor were they in early 1973
just before the most recent decline got under way. We did point
out in our reports at the time that the abrupt demise of Phase II
of President Nixon's economic controls program probably meant
more inflation. We recognized that this could upset the market,
and we further suggested, "For those with idle funds, some slowdown in new buying for a while should suffice. However, for the
fully invested, a sale or two here to build a bit of insurance is
worth considering."

Of course, the inflationary explosion that came along was much
worse than we or anyone else expected, and scared the spots off
the stock market.

While we missed the degree of inflationary heat, we failed
altogether to anticipate the effects of Watergate and the Equity
Funding adventure. The Watergate bugging attempt blew into
the biggest political scandal in the nation's history, upsetting
investors and voters alike, not to mention bankers and bureau-

crats both here and abroad. The Equity Funding phantom insurance caper will prove to be, many believe, the biggest heist ever pulled off in the corporate world.

THE WISE ARE WARY

It should be obvious to all that such things as these cannot be forecast. For this reason, prudent investment advisers are reluctant to jump to extreme positions. The risks of precipitate action are high and the penalties of error great.

On the other hand, if you concentrate your clients' holdings in good, solid companies it is almost impossible to lose, long term. Certainly, good stocks go down with everything else in bear markets, but they don't stay down. Take Exxon. It dropped from 85 to 50 in 1969–70. By early 1973 it was bumping 100 and even now is 90. Thus, anyone who had sold Exxon at the top in 1970 would not be a nickel ahead today.

To suggest that the Exxon seller at the top in 1970 would have bought back near the bottom in the same year is to dream. After a long time in this business, we can say that people, professional or amateur, generally don't. Once out of a given issue they tend to stay out.

So neither we nor any other long-term investment advisers are likely to switch you from stocks to cash and back to stocks again as our views of the probable trend of stock prices change. That is why the mutual fund industry, which reported $3 billion in cash at the end of 1972, reported approximately the same figure toward the end of 1975. The cash figure ran higher and lower during that three-year period, but at no time did it come to a significant percentage of this $40 billion industry. The range most of the time was between 6% and 12%, nowhere near the 25% or 50% that would be needed if these institutions were really trying to take advantage of market swings. The same may be said for the big bank trust departments. Morgan Guaranty, for example, the biggest of all, is always almost fully invested in such common stocks as IBM, Eastman Kodak, and the like.

STAY WITH THE BEST ONES

As it is easy to see, these have been among the best performers in recent years. Obviously, if Morgan Guaranty had followed the policy our letter writer suggested, of selling on the way up, these probably would have been the issues selected.

Similarly, if you were to review the holdings of major mutual funds and pension plans, you would find the same stocks predominating. One can only conclude from the evidence that investors with the most money and most experience tend to stay fully invested in the best stocks most of the time.

Our response to the criticism is this, then. While we may suggest an investor lighten his stock load at critical junctures in the stock market, our main aim is to keep him in the best stocks. We know from experience that they will rise more than they will fall, thereby ensuring the growth of his savings over the long pull.

We still think this is good advice. Don't try to beat the market. Don't believe that you can outsmart everyone else. Simply accept the fact that stock prices always fluctuate and that they usually move up and down to the complete (but perhaps not admitted!) surprise of investors, amateur and professional alike.

AVERAGING DOWN

Advantage can be taken of the cycles in stock prices, however. For example, let's suppose you buy a promising but volatile growth stock such as Perkin-Elmer at 40 only to see a major market shakeout come along that tumbles the stock down to 25. It's worth noting that Perkin-Elmer, in going from the equivalent of 7 in 1961 (it has been through three two-for-one splits since) to present levels in the 20s, has twice dropped more than 50% in 1961–62 and again in 1969–70. (Note chart.) A 25% drop is easy!

Now you as a holder of Perkin-Elmer have a few extra dollars retrieved from your spending stream (or, more properly, your family's spending stream) to invest. Why not buy more Perkin-

PERKIN-ELMER CORP. (PKN)

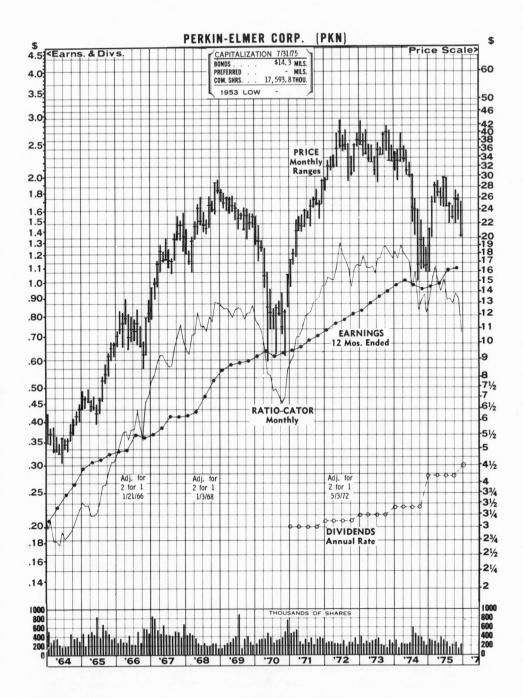

CAPITALIZATION 7/31/75
BONDS . . . . $14.3 MILS.
PREFERRED . . - MILS.
COM. SHRS. . . 17,593.8 THOU.
1953 LOW -

Earns. & Divs.   Price Scale>

PRICE
Monthly
Ranges

EARNINGS
12 Mos. Ended

RATIO-CATOR
Monthly

Adj. for
2 for 1
1/21/66

Adj. for
2 for 1
1/3/68

Adj. for
2 for 1
5/3/72

DIVIDENDS
Annual Rate

THOUSANDS OF SHARES

'64 '65 '66 '67 '68 '69 '70 '71 '72 '73 '74 '75

Chart by Securities Research Co., 208 Newbury Street,
Boston, Mass. 02116

Elmer while it is down? The stock is off because the market as a whole is off. The Arabs have acted up or the Fed has tightened money. Something has happened to scare the market, but nothing has occurred to reduce the investment merit of Perkin-Elmer. So you buy more. You have averaged down. The cost of your old shares has been reduced by "averaging" that cost with the figure paid for the new shares.

TAKING PART PROFITS

If it's wise to put more money into your favorite stock when it is down, shouldn't you sell a part of same when it is way up? As we indicated earlier in the chapter, our answer generally is no. If you sell all or part you probably won't buy it back—people just never seem to.

And if you put the money in another stock, which appears cheaper anyway, you'll probably find that it goes down as well as the one you hold. You've merely incurred a capital gains tax that you didn't need! If you are going to sell a stock, do so because you question the long-run nature of the business.

It's perfectly okay to wait for a generally strong market before disposing of such an issue. But don't try to nip a profit here and there among your Xeroxes and Eastman Kodaks, for you probably will end up with fewer of the very shares you want. It's tough to outsmart all the CFAs around the country who spend so much time and money trying, futilely, to outsmart each other.

Don't forget. If you just play along at the University of Chicago's "proven" rate of 9% per year compounded, you will double your savings dollar every eight years. That ain't hay!

JUST SURVIVAL . . .

Anyone who has been around long enough to survive a couple of complete market cycles often suspects that ninety percent of the battle is to survive market collapses. No matter how long your

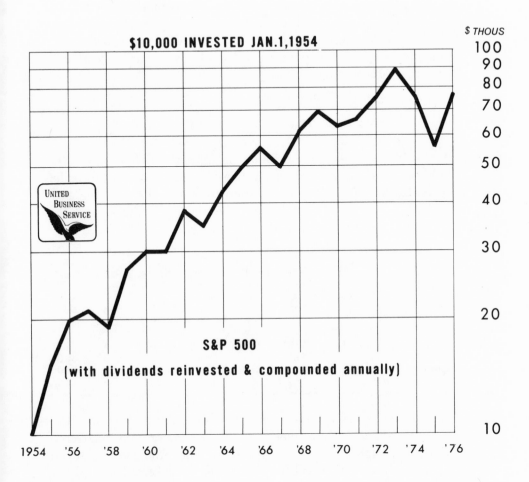

$10,000 INVESTED JAN.1,1954

$ THOUS

100
90
80
70
60
50
40
30
20
10

UNITED
BUSINESS
SERVICE

S&P 500

(with dividends reinvested & compounded annually)

1954   '56   '58   '60   '62   '64   '66   '68   '70   '72   '74   '76

Source: Standard & Poor's

experience and how keen your mind, bear markets invariably catch you by surprise.

So rather than trying to outsmart the unoutsmartable or predict the unpredictable, most sophisticated investors stick to good-quality stocks, confident in the knowledge that when someone or something "pulls the plug," these stocks will decline least and eventually recover most.

. . . IS THE NAME OF THE GAME

For evidence consider the following figures which compare the "old-favorite averages" with the more "sophisticated" or broader compilations. The Dow-Jones Industrial Average and the S&P Industrials represent the former, the Indicator Digest and the Value Line Composite the latter.

	% Decline Dec. '68– May '70	% Rise May '70– Apr. '71	% Decline Apr. '71– Nov. '71	% Rise Nov. '71– Jan. '73	% Decline Jan. '73– Dec. '73	% Rise Dec. '73– Mar. '74	% Decline Dec. '68– Dec. '74
DJIA	34.1	50.6	16.1	31.8	25.0	11.4	34.7
S&P Industrials	36.0	53.3	14.2	35.4	23.2	5.3	32.3
Indicator Digest	54.1	54.1	21.7	17.3	40.1	11.9	74.0
Value Line Comp.	54.9	48.0	22.6	18.7	38.9	15.5	72.0

The differences in performance are painfully easy to see. The broader averages have consistently lost more and recovered less all through the seesaw years since 1968. And most seasoned investors believe this will be the case in the future. Hence, their affinity for the tried and true when it comes to stocks.

20

Shortcuts to Riches (and Ruin)

We humans are greedy. Few among us don't long for easy riches, something for nothing. Our main differences are that some will take more of a chance than others. The Tommy Manvilles* will go from bride to bride seeking marital bliss at the risk of public divorce and private rancor while the confirmed bachelors move cautiously along a narrow risk-free track. So also in the world of securities, the stock market speculator will reach for big gains at the risk of big losses while the rest of us tiptoe along with Mother Bell.

If you are a financial Tommy Manville, if you can take a chance and still sleep nights or, more important, take a loss without qualm, you might well look into such shortcuts as warrants, short sales, margin buying, and the latest fad in legal gambling—options. All of these magnify the action of the stock market enormously. Up or down, these things always get there faster. Let's take stock warrants first.

---

* For younger readers, Tommy Manville was heir to the Johns-Manville fortune and spent much of the 1920s, 1930s, and 1940s going through eleven wives, at least as many legal suits, and umpteen millions of his inherited dollars.

STOCK WARRANTS—INSTANT ACTION

A stock warrant is a call on a particular stock. It gives you the opportunity to buy a stock at a predetermined price. Sometimes the call is limited in time such as were the American Telephone warrants, sometimes they are good forever. Of course, the shorter the life of the warrant the less the value.

Take the Telephone warrants. Issued in May 1970 to "sweeten" an otherwise ho-hum offering of 8.75% debentures, these warrants allowed holders to buy the common at a price of 52 up until May 15, 1975. Obviously, as American Telephone common traded on the open market at 50, the warrants had little real value. However, they did sell for a few dollars as a speculator's bet that the common one day would sell at 60 or more.

IT'S LEVERAGE THAT DOES IT

If you are the timid type and hold Telephone as it goes from 50 to 55, you enjoy a gain of 10%. But if you own the warrants you would likely see them go from 5 to 9, representing a profit of 80%, or eight times what you won on the common. On the other hand, many buyers of the warrants paid between 9 and 10 for them early in 1973. By midyear they were selling just under 5, a plunge of about 50%, while the common declined by only 15%.

So the American Telephone warrants offer you a much greater profit opportunity than the common does, with the assurance that if the stock retreats, they will collapse. The risk is heightened by their relatively brief life. In this case the common drifted along just under the exercise price, and as the expiration date approached the warrants slid slowly to zero.

JUST A CALL ON THE FUTURE

It is well to remember also that warrants have no equity in assets or earnings and, of course, receive no dividends. No one should buy a warrant unless he also likes the outlook for the common stock on which it gives him a call. And it is best to avoid warrants with nearby expirations and those where the stock is selling far below the exercise price. What gives warrants their allure is the possibility of large percentage gains. What should give you pause is the demonstrably large risk that goes along with them.

To give you an idea of the volatility you can expect with warrants, compared with that of common stock, note the figures in the following table.

| | % DECLINE FROM 1968–69 HIGH | | % REBOUND TO 1973 HIGH | |
	Warrant	Stock	Warrant	Stock
Fibreboard	70	61	50	35
Indian Head	83	70	120	93
Kaufman & Broad	64	57	289	100
Loews Corp.	85	74	217	200
Tenneco, Inc.	73	48	200	76
Textron, Inc.	86	74	257	127
Warner Communications	60	53	250	86

SHORT SELLING

This is a procedure that allows the investor—or rather, speculator—to borrow a stock from his broker and then sell it on the open market. He does this when he thinks the stock in question, or perhaps the entire market, is headed down. He hopes to repay his loan to the broker by repurchasing the stock at lower prices and returning the stock certificate to him.

It works this way. Let's suppose you had watched Polaroid move up to an all-time record price of 130 in 1969, to a price-earnings ratio of equally record proportions. Because the company's earnings growth had slowed, you decided that the stock was overpriced. Being a speculator of strong heart, you borrowed 100 shares from your broker and promptly sold them for $13,000. The stock subsequently rose a little into the 140s and then plummeted to the 50s the following year, mid-1970. Still dreaming, let's further suppose you bought 100 shares then for $5,800 and returned the certificate to your broker. Your profit was the difference between the two figures, less some very minor expenses, or about $7,000. This amounts to a gain of 55% in a matter of months. Not bad!

Suppose, to give you the other side of the coin, you had done the same in 1963 when Polaroid enjoyed a similarly sharp run-up and achieved a record-breaking P/E. Again, earnings growth was slowing. Suppose you sold short at 22, close to the high. You would have seen the issue dropping briefly to 18 or 19 only to soar to 125 before it rested. If you lost your nerve and covered then—bought the stock back—you would have paid $12,000 to repay a $2,200 loan for a loss of $9,800, or some 450%. Had you waited long enough, you could have easily covered at 140 for a 540% loss.

The fact of the matter is, losses on the long side, where you simply go out and buy a stock, are limited to the amount invested—and stocks rarely go to zero. But on the short side, the sky is literally the limit as far as losses are concerned. If you are inclined to gamble and feel like selling short, remember this hoary couplet:

> He who sells what isn't his'n
> Must buy it back or go to prison.

10% DOWN WILL DO

Back in 1929, in the halcyon days of stock market gambling, you could buy stocks with a 10% margin, or down payment. The remaining 90% you borrowed from your friendly broker. He made the commissions on your transactions plus interest on the loans you carried. You took the profits—or losses.

This proved so disastrous that the Federal Reserve Board took over control of margins and nowadays keeps them somewhere between 50% and 80%, a far cry from 10%! But even in this area you can singe your fingers, if not actually lose your shirt. Suppose, again, that you bought an attractive but volatile growth stock such as Perkin-Elmer back in 1968 at 24, on a margin of

65%. This meant that you put up about $1,500 and borrowed $900 from your broker. The stock subsequently moved modestly ahead to the high 20s and then slid steadily back to 24.

Then along came the 1969–70 market decline and Perkin-Elmer collapsed into the teens. Being rightfully more interested in his own financial skin than yours, your broker would have suggested you put up more cash, as the price approached his $900 loan. If you can recall the panicky fears of that market crash—the Dow fell 20 points on May 25, Blue Monday—you know that you might have hesitated to throw good money after bad. You could well have told your man to sell, collect his loan, and send you whatever crumbs were left. Your loss would have been nearly 40%. Yet if you had not been forced to sell, if you had been able to hang on, you would have seen your holdings of Perkin-Elmer come right back to your cost and then nearly double.

In short, the risk in margin buying is that you may be forced to sell at the wrong time. The appeal of margin buying is that you can use your broker's money to make profits for you. If, in the preceding example, you had sold Perkin-Elmer at a modest profit when it got to 28 shortly after you bought it, your profit would have been only $400. But on *your* investment of $1,500, that $400 represents a gain of more than 25%. Pretty good. The fact is, margin buying is risky, as are short sales and warrants. They are only for the stouthearted.

NOW FOR OPTIONS

As if investors could not lose their shirts fast enough with specu- lation on margin or short selling, three new option markets offer an even quicker way to riches or ruin. The Chicago Board Op- tions Exchange originated the option market, followed by the American and Philadelphia-Baltimore-Washington Exchanges. Now the Big Board is eyeing this lucrative field.

All this means is that for a few dollars you can buy a call and, theoretically, make a killing on a small move in the stock underly- ing your option. For example, an option on American Telephone may move from 1 to 2, or 100%, while the stock itself advances only 20%. This is the same type of action you can get in warrants, only infinitely more so. One day a 4% rise in Eastman Kodak common caused the option to triple!

As one enthusiast said, options limit your losses to 100%—of a very small number of dollars. So some people rush in where they should fear to tread. Trading in options lets them trade in IBM, Kodak, Xerox, etc., on a "two-bit" basis. It remains to be seen if such trading produces any real profits. At the risk of sounding very proper Bostonian, we believe this to be more entertainment than investment, and expensive at that. But, if you want to put a small amount in options while the rest of your portfolio is solidly invested in good stocks and bonds, we can hardly complain.

Let's consider an example. Suppose you like Hewlett-Packard, which has come down from 120 to 92. You think the stock's oversold. You rate it a "buy," but you don't have enough money to purchase 100 shares. Don't be depressed. You can obtain an option on 100 shares on the CBOE—at the time of this writing, for $500.

The option gives you the right to buy 100 shares of Hewlett at 100, 8 points above the market. The option is good for five months. If the stock returns to 120 as you expect it to, you will have a $1,500 gain—the difference between 100, your option price, and 120 less your investment of $500. This would be a profit of 200%. If you had purchased the shares outright at the market, 92, your gain would have been more in points, 28, but less in percent, 30%, not quite one sixth of your option gain. Even if you had bought the stock on a 50% margin, your gain would have been only 60%, little more than a fourth of your option profit.

Here's the way this looks in figures:

	Price	Cost	Sell Price	Amount Realized from Sale	PROFIT $	%
100 Hewlett-Packard	92	$9,200	$120	$12,000	2,800	+30
100 Hewlett (50% margin)	92	4,600	120	12,000	2,800*	+60
100 Hewlett option	100	500	120	2,000	1,500	+200

* Less interest on the broker's loan.

LOSSES ARE EASY, TOO

Pretty impressive figures, aren't they? Now, if the stock does not rally as you expect, your maximum loss is $500, which is small in dollars, but big in percent—100%! Furthermore, losses are easy to suffer because of the time limit on the option. Of course, you can salvage something by selling early. In truth, most option traders don't anticipate exercising the contract. But, without some up-move in the underlying stock, the option premium will remain constant or drop and the trader will be left holding the proverbial bag. However, as pointed out above, the loss may be cut by closing out the position before the option expires and becomes worthless.

Then, too, the stock has to rally during the life of the option. In the foregoing example, a rally in Hewlett after the five-month life of the option brings no charm or profit.

OPTIONS CAN BE SOLD, TOO

So much for the purchase of options, which is simply buying a call, the right to buy a particular stock at a certain price within a definite time period. How about *selling* options? Is this a way to instant riches?

The answer must be a qualified yes. With luck, one can profit by selling options, albeit much more modestly and at much less risk. Going back to Hewlett, let's suppose you own 100 shares at a current price of 92. You sell through the CBOE, giving some other investor a chance to buy your stock at 100 within 150 days. For illustration, say you get $500 for the option. If the stock fails to reach 100 or better during the life of the option contract, the right to buy is not exercised, naturally. So you still have your 100 shares, plus the $500, and are ready to sell another option.

Suppose the stock does rally sharply above 100 and the option is exercised. You get $10,000 for the stock plus the $500 from the option, or $10,500. That's $1,300 more than the $9,200 the stock was worth when you sold the option. The only trouble is, you no longer have the stock. But you can promptly remedy this by re-buying on the open market—albeit at a somewhat higher price, presumably. Or, you can buy in your option to close out the position and then repeat the process by selling a new option expiring six months further out.

HURRAY FOR THE BROKERS

In addition to the modest gains you take on a rising stock in selling options, you also get the dividends. With many of the underlying common stocks, this amounts to 5% or better. So the appeal here is considerable. We might add, however, that though it is win, lose, or draw for you, it is only win, win, win for the broker. All transactions, purchases and sales, are completed within 90 days or less, and then repeated. For the brokers this is plain heaven.

Option exchanges are still very new. Only 135 common stocks were on their option lists as of the end of 1975. Yet volume amounted to about 10% of the volume of trading on the "Big Board," no mean feat for so new a venture. So option trading is an impressive innovation in the financial firmament.

Most of the trading is being done by institutions for market stabilizing, hedging, and other such reasons. Thus, it is not the terrain for any but the most sophisticated and well-heeled individual investors.

21

Dollar Cost Averaging

No discussion of market timing can be complete without some comment on the so-called dollar cost averaging approach, which assumes regular investment of a fixed number of dollars in a specified stock or stocks. Just about every other market timing guide or technique is premised on the assumption that human judgment aided by proper experience and good information can help the investor "buy them low and sell them high," which, after all, is the route to stock market profits.

But not dollar cost averaging. The assumption here is that human judgment will err more often than not. Thus, the way around the dilemma of determining when stocks are high and when they're low is to buy stocks regularly without regard for price levels. Anyone who does this will soon find that he is paying some frighteningly lofty prices at times, but at others he will really be getting a "steal." And if the amount of money invested is held constant, the arithmetic guarantees that you will buy more shares at the bottom than at the top.

HOW TO BEAT THE MARKET

By way of example, let's suppose you had purchased $1,000 worth of Standard Oil of Indiana in January of each of the past five years. Here's how it would look in figures:

	Amount	Price*	Shares Bought*
Jan. 1971	$1,000	29	34.5
Jan. 1972	1,000	34	29.4
Jan. 1973	1,000	45	22.2
Jan. 1974	1,000	46	21.7
Jan. 1975	1,000	41	24.4
		39 Av.	132.2

Value, December 1975 = $5,685

* Adjusted for stock split.

Even after you had bought your fourth installment close to an all-time high and had weathered the rather sharp decline brought on by the Middle East oil embargo, you still showed a 14% profit. Of course, the picture would have looked much better if you had picked a more dynamic growth stock such as Caterpillar Tractor, which gained 31% in the same time period, or Dow Chemical, which increased in value by 115%!

NOTHING IS CERTAIN

Conversely, the picture would look worse if you had picked a stock that went down in the 1969–70 bear market and stayed there. But while it is very difficult to pick market lows, it is not impossible to pick stocks that trend upward over the long pull, reflecting corporate growth about in line with that of the economy.

This method merely entails the regular investment, at any interval (monthly, quarterly, or annually), of any reasonable amount ($50, $100, $500, or whatever), regardless of stock market or business conditions. In short, you rule out the vagaries of human judgment in market timing, using your brains only to select the stocks to be bought in the first place.

One investor we know used the New York Stock Exchange's Monthly Investment Plan, which allows for the purchase of fractional shares, to buy three stocks quarterly. He invested $50 per month this way for a number of years in three leading growth stocks and did very well.

Stock A was bought in January, B in February, C in March, and then A again in April and so on. This gave him a pretty well diversified investment program at the very start. Each of the companies was broadly diversified, so the three of them gave him representation in a wide area of industrial activity immediately.

Other investors prefer to concentrate in one stock. They like to see the number of shares build up more rapidly. That is okay, of course, but being essentially conservative ourselves, we incline to the "instant" diversification approach.

When it comes to specific stocks to buy this way we can approve about any blue chip, respectable growth stock, or even some carefully selected "red" chips with real growth potential. Just about any issue mentioned so far in this book would be suitable, although the strictly income recommendations would be of least attraction.

22

On Beating the Market

Many investors enjoy trying to beat the market even if they know in their hearts that they probably can't. But if life is essentially a game, they ask, why shouldn't investing be, too? So they hunt around for things to buy that others have either overlooked or failed to comprehend when they did see them.

SPECIAL SITUATIONS

One group of such stocks is called "special situations." A special situation can be one of many things; a take-over candidate, for example, or a company under new management about to move in exciting and more profitable directions. It can also develop as the result of a research breakthrough or a highly promising product introduction. In general, these are issues with delayed profit potentials whose future performance will be governed more by internal developments than the action of the overall market.

It should be enlightening to review some examples from the past. Early in 1972, the Kendall Company, a Massachusetts-based hospital and medical supply company with a good record, caught the fancy of a couple of major national corporations, Textron and Colgate-Palmolive. Kendall stock had been selling in the low 40s for nearly a year, at a rather high P/E of 24. No bargain.

However, as soon as the company's suitors began bidding for her favors, Kendall's stock shot up 10 points to the low 50s. Finally, when Colgate made its successful offer in March, Kendall common was up to 59, a good third above its January level. The offer was a share-for-share exchange with Colgate common at 65. This, of course, gave Kendall holders another 6 points. The moral: merger candidates have special appeal.

CHANGING THE LEOPARD'S SPOTS

Another type of special situation occurs when a company spins off a major subsidiary. Often the parts are worth more than the whole. This, of course, is just the opposite of what happened in the Kendall-Colgate story just related.

For a variety of reasons, Georgia-Pacific management decided in 1972 to divest itself of a sizable part of its timber and manufacturing assets in the form of a new company, Louisiana Pacific. When all was said and done, the new corporation would be remarkably akin to its parent, a forest products company.

Georgia-Pacific's common had been doing little prior to the announcement of the intended spin-off. The stock was selling at about 36 when the news broke in mid-October and promptly went to 40 by the end of the month. At the end of November the stock closed at 43, representing a gain of about 20% in a matter of six weeks.

A year later Georgia-Pacific sold at 40 again while its offspring, Louisiana Pacific, sold at 42, giving the original buyer of Georgia-Pacific at 36 in October of 1972 a combined value (one share of Georgia-Pacific and one-fifth share of Louisiana Pacific) in October 1973 of 49, for a profit of 35%. During this 12-month period the market, as measured by the Dow Industrials, did not budge. The moral: split-ups are every bit as good for stockholders as mergers—if you buy in advance.

NEW PRODUCTS HELP

Williams Companies has been a profitable special situation twice
in a decade, no mean feat. The company was in the pipeline
construction business in the early 1960s, and not very profitably,
at that. Earnings per share hit a low of 15¢ in 1964 and the 19¢
dividend was passed. Looking for more promising areas in which
to function the company bought a pipeline in the Midwest from a
group of oil companies that had wearied of a regulated interstate
common-carrier business. They reasoned that they could use the
money much more profitably exploring for and producing oil.

So they sold out to Williams and the new owner promptly
made the pipeline pay. Williams common, which sank nearly to 2
in 1964, climbed slowly to 4 in August of 1965 and soared to 22 in
the final quarter of the year.

A few years later, in 1971, Williams bought Gulf's fertilizer
business and the next year acquired that of Continental Oil.
Curiously enough, these two oil companies had gone into the
fertilizer business to prosper from the massive increase in food
demand expected from a burgeoning world population. But it
hadn't developed as expected and the big oil companies lost

PROFITS MADE ON HISTORIC SPECIAL SITUATIONS

Stock	Type of Special Situation	% Profit	Period Involved
Loew's Theaters	Hidden assets	450	1 year
Pittston	Undervalued assets	212	2 years
Englehard Minerals	Undervalued earnings	296	2 years
Leasco Data Processing	Management policy	315	1 year
Kresge	Management policy	318	2 years
Fedders	Management policy	281	1 year
White Consolidated	Mergers & acquisitions	237	2 years
Polaroid	New product development	298	1 year
Teledyne	Mergers & consolidations	492	1 year
Sperry Rand	Management policy	485	2 years
U.S. Industries	Mergers & consolidations	256	1 year
Kerr-McGee	Hidden assets	236	2 years
Raytheon	Management policy	203	1 year
Hilton Hotels	Undervalued assets	395	1 year
Jim Walter	Management policy	206	1 year
Xerox	New Product Development	284	2 years

patience. So Williams bought and for a couple of years little happened. Then came the food price explosion of 1973. Williams common, which had hovered around 40–45 for 1971, 1972, and much of 1973, soared to 70 in the last quarter of 1973. The moral: profitable new products make stock market gains.

The preceding table lists some other intriguing special situations that *Forbes* magazine reported on—after the fact, they hastened to state—a few years ago.

There's no question that special situations occur. It's just the finding of them that's tough. And then when you do find one you may have to exercise a lot of patience. You may find it easier simply to buy good growth stocks.

23

Tax Shelters: Proceed with Caution

In contemplating your own tax and investment posture, no doubt you have given thought to so-called tax shelters. Judging from the flood of such deals (oil and gas exploration and drilling, real estate, agricultural programs—cattle feeding, cattle breeding, etc.—timberland, vineyards, and equipment leasing, etc.) seeking SEC regulation, the temptation to participate will increase. Sometimes tax shelters are a real help; more often, they are not. Here is a brief guide to their use. We hope you'll pardon our cautionary view of them.

First of all, a tax shelter is not a "loophole." Tax shelters are deliberate legislative creations designed to channel private investment money into areas of national need by offering certain tax incentives. A loophole is a legislative oversight through which tax savings sometimes can be achieved.

RIFE WITH REEFS

Tax shelters are popular for the obvious reason that they can use for personal investment money that would otherwise go to the government, hopefully generating tax-free income and/or tax losses that can shelter other income. Also, in some cases, returns can be classified as capital gains instead of ordinary income and thus be taxed at more favorable rates.

There are several disadvantages to investment in tax shelters, and you should be fully aware of them before embarking on a tax shelter program of your own. First, many of them carry a high degree of risk. Your chances of reaping any return at all in some cases are minimal, in other cases marginal. Second, they are generally rather illiquid; you cannot easily get your assets out of the investment, or you must make a long-term commitment. Third, they are targets for swindle. Though publicly offered programs must be registered with the SEC, regulation is generally much more lax than in other investment areas. Private programs are even more susceptible to hanky-panky. This does not mean that all tax shelter programs are fraudulent, but it does mean that you must be certain that you are dealing with reputable individuals if you elect to participate.

Tax shelter packages are set up as limited partnerships. You, the investor, are the "limited" partner, which means that your liability is limited only to the extent of your investment. As a member of a partnership you take any tax consequences on your own individual return. A "general" partner puts the deal together, provides the expertise and management, and usually charges, besides a management fee, a percentage of the action. While you can lose your entire stake, the general partner rarely loses, for he collects his management fee whether the venture succeeds or not. If it makes the big time, you both win big, but he usually wins bigger than you.

While they are not the exclusive fief of the wealthy, tax shelters hold the most potential benefit for those in the higher tax brackets. However, with their growing popularity, the market of available tax shelter options is expanding.

OIL: A STACKED DECK

In the case of oil participations, in many respects you're playing with the deck stacked against you. First, most of the "easy" oil has been found. Second, if there is a reasonably good chance of finding oil, the driller will try to finance the project himself so he won't have to share the profits. That leaves you with the hard-to-get stuff. The odds are borne out by the fact that only one wildcat well in ten yields any oil, and even that might not be in sufficient quantity to be profitable.

But once in a while the "big one" comes in, and the return can be sizable. Then, too, most of the cost of the drilling can be tax deductible. Total cost of a dry well can be deducted. Oil from wells that produce can be partially protected by the depletion allowance.

REAL ESTATE: A GAME FOR EXPERTS

Real estate is the most popular form of tax shelter, for a variety of reasons. One is that there is considerable opportunity for heavy tax write-offs during the early years of participation. After that, deductions continue, though at a declining rate. Also, real estate investment affords attractive leverage—up to 80% can be borrowed in most instances—and full deductions can be applied against the investor's 20% stake. In the case of some FHA projects, up to 90% can be borrowed on a 40-year mortgage.

Another reason for popularity is that real estate investments *can* be relatively safe, providing they are properly executed to begin with, are properly managed and continuously occupied.

A widely used vehicle for group investment is a limited partnership called a real estate syndicate. So popular have syndicates become that more than a few hastily assembled, shoddily constructed, and inefficiently managed projects have begun to backfire on their investors. Unless you are a specialist in real estate, you probably would do better to place your assets elsewhere.

TARGET FOR REFORM

Will tax "reform" eliminate shelters? It's too early to tell. There is a certain amount of pressure for this, particularly in some areas such as oil, gas, and mineral depletion allowances. There also might be some more restricting of real estate shelters. The 1969 Tax Reform Law did a considerable amount of tightening up— eliminating citrus groves altogether, curtailing benefits in cattle breeding and feeding, reducing benefits for oil and mineral exploration, modifying capital gains provisions, and cutting oil depletion allowances. Thus, the trend has been established and the national mood seems to be leaning toward more restrictions, so the value of tax shelters as an investment planning tool might be diminishing.

Besides the "fatherly advice" we've already given you, here are a few more pointers. Be extremely careful with whom you deal. Beyond that, be sure your losses will really shelter other income and that any losses will not unduly damage your financial position. Tax considerations, as in most other investments, should be secondary—your first concern should be the soundness of the investment. Don't be like the foolish investor who sold off a portfolio of solid but unspectacular common stocks and put the entire proceeds into an oil drilling venture that went broke, carrying him from riches to rags in the process. Seek competent counsel. Consult your tax adviser to make sure a tax shelter can indeed help your investment posture. He can also help you weigh the risks against the potential returns, and make sure that your tax "savings" do not generate unwanted tax liability.

Fitting Investments into Your Total Financial Planning Picture

THE BACK YARD

The Women's Lib girls have a point when they decry the extra hurdles they have to contend with. But things used to be worse. Note how this Colonial will treated the loyal wife who had labored long and hard alongside her mate to make the family what it was.

"I give unto Elizabeth Burbank, my well beloved wife, the use and improvement of one half of my Dwelling House, and one of the Cellars under the House whilst she remains my widow and I will that my Executor provide for her yearly one hundred pounds of Port one hundred pounds of Beef three Barrells of Cyder Eight Bushells of Indian Corn three Bushells of Rie two Bushells of wheat one Bushell and a half of Malt one Bushell of Salt ten pounds of Sheeps Wool, fifteen pounds of Flax, Sufficient fire wood cut for the fire at the Door, Seven pounds of Sugar one Gallon of Rum, two pairs of Shoes, Six Bushells of Apples twelve pounds of Tobacco, and a sufficient quantity of Sauce of every sort: Also I will that my Executor provide a Horse for her to Ride when she shall have occasion for it; and I give her the use of a Cow; and I will that my Executor keep her well summer and winter for the use of my wife so long as she remains my widow."

At best she got only half her home, and if she remarried she was to lose it all. No wonder there has been so much zip to the Women's Lib movement from Susan B. Anthony to Gloria Steinem.

July 23, 1973

24

Financing College and the Golden Years

This section of the book is designed to show you how to get the most out of your personal finances. It goes a bit beyond the security markets and simultaneously tries to bear down on specific subjects, problems, and predicaments that are likely to confront a number of mortal investors. First, the matters of educating your offspring and preparing for retirement.

IS YOUR WALLET READY FOR COLLEGE?

For those who haven't priced a college education lately, some shock is in store. As I write this book, I can attest that a year in the average institution of higher learning runs around $5,000. This does not count a "set of wheels" for the little fellow or gal, either. It is slightly more than the bare bones of tuition, room, board, books, and blue jeans.

With the tab rising by 5%–7% a year, a sheepskin that costs $20,000 today could well bear a price tag of $35,000 or more by the 1980s. Even if your babe's still in arms it's not too soon to start planning. Actually, as we have pointed out earlier in this book, it is not only better to start sooner, but when dealing with the stock market, better to start sooner or not at all. The market jumps around too much to put tuition money into common stocks three or four years before the bill comes in. It might be your luck to have Wall Street come unglued just before the start of the second semester.

You've got two jobs: first, to set aside some funds; second, to make sure these funds work as hard as possible for you while they're waiting to go to college.

A portfolio of about $10,000 in growth stocks should appreciate sufficiently in value in the next decade to meet a large share of the costs at a "prestige" college. Such an investment program might look like this:

FUND FOR A COLLEGE EDUCATION

No. of Shares		Dec. 1975 Price	Cost	Dividend	Annual Income
40	Abbott Labs	41	$ 1,640	$0.80	$ 32
40	Citicorp	29	1,160	0.88	35
40	Continental Oil	58	2,320	2.00	80
40	Federated Department Stores	54	2,160	1.24	50
40	General Electric	49	1,960	1.60	64
40	Stanley Works	21	840	1.04	42
			$10,080		$303

Or you might prefer to set aside some funds on a regular basis. Such a program takes discipline, but it can pay off handsomely. For instance, if you had invested as little as $200 each birthday since your child was one year old in 1957 in a growth stock like Abbott and plowed back all dividends, the $3,600 cost would be worth about $10,500 today as he gets ready to go off to school. By increasing the yearly contribution as your earnings rose, you could have accumulated enough to pay the entire cost of college.

Remember, the earlier you start planning for your children's education, the easier the annual burden will be—and the greater the benefits from capital appreciation of good investments.

SHORT-TERM TRUST AS A TAX SHELTER

You hear a lot about short-term trusts in connection with planning ahead to finance a college education. They're also called ten-year trusts, reversionary trusts, or Clifford trusts, and they can be a useful tool, if properly set up and operated. Recent tax law changes have somewhat diluted their effectiveness, but did not do irreparable harm.

The basic aim of the trusts is to provide a tax shelter for parents in high-income tax brackets, but they can be established by parents who expect to enter the earnings stratosphere later in their careers, and they also can serve as vehicles for an orderly, systematic investment program.

The short-term trust allows parents to shift investment income to family members with lower tax liabilities—namely, minor children. Income earned by assets of the trust is taxed at, say, 15% rather than 50%, or 35%, or even 25%. Then, after at least ten years, assets revert to the parents.

To obtain the most tax leverage, such a trust must be set up fairly early in a child's life; age six or younger is ideal. If the child is within two or three years of college, you might as well forget it; the trust probably won't help much.

Here's how it is frequently used. Income-producing assets are transferred to the trust. The minor child is named beneficiary, and anyone other than the donor is named trustee. Otherwise, if the donor should die before the trust expires, its assets could be regarded as part of his estate and taxed as such.

The trustee should distribute all income currently. This current income is deposited into a savings account or certificate of deposit in the child's name. Someone other than the donor should act as custodian of the account. Compliance with the Uniform Gift to Minors Act should be assured—a point the donor's attorney should be sure to check on.

To ensure maximum tax advantage, two years before the child enters college all income in the custodial account is converted into a two-year certificate of deposit. When the CD matures, sufficient principal is transferred to a special checking account for the child's first-year college expenses. The balance of the principal is put into another CD maturing the following year, and the interest from both CDs is put back into the child's savings account. All income earned during the college years should be kept out of the account for expenses.

All this jockeying is necessary to assure that current-year income is separated from funds used to pay college expenses, since income from a custodial account used to support a minor child is taxed to the parent.

This is clearly a job for a qualified tax and legal adviser. He can also steer you away from shoals that might be present in your own state's statutory structure.

BORROWING FOR COLLEGE

If you haven't salted away enough cash, you will probably have to borrow to meet college expenses. Most savings institutions have tuition loan plans, but they can be burdensome. Typically, in 1973 you could get up to $15,000 for up to six years at going interest rates.

On the other hand, you might be able to obtain a federally guaranteed loan, with an interest rate ceiling substantially lower than the "free-market" rate. Since these rules have had a tendency to change frequently, your best bet would be to check with your state's guarantee agency or with your local bank for the program's current status.

INVESTING FOR RETIREMENT

If education always costs more, so does retirement, especially in these inflationary times. This problem is particularly difficult for the self-employed—the doctor, dentist, lawyer, or anyone whose pension problems are not solved automatically by his or her corporate big brother.

The government has reached out to help the self-employed in

recent years through the Keogh program. At the start, back in 1962, the opportunities for tax shelter were rather modest and paled before the magnanimous munificence of the average corporate plan. But over the years they have been liberalized, and in 1974 Congress took a major step toward equalizing the tax break. Thus, Keogh is well worth considering in your retirement program if you work for yourself.

HOW KEOGH WORKS

Under HR 10, as Keogh is also known, a self-employed person can set aside in a "qualified" plan and take as a tax deduction the lesser of 15% of his earned income or $7,500 in any tax year (up from the 10% or $2,500 limits provided before the law was amended). Dividends and capital gains are reinvested and escape taxes until benefits start to be drawn. They are then taxed as ordinary income, but presumably in a much lower tax bracket than in prime earning years.

Who qualifies? Basically, you're eligible if you pay your own social security taxes in full. Here's another point: Even if you are employed by someone else but earn a substantial amount of money on the side through, say, consulting work, you can establish a Keogh plan based on these outside earnings.

If you have full-time employees with more than three years of service, you must include them in your plan. Contributions you make for them (but not for yourself) are fully deductible business expenses.

THERE ARE PITFALLS

The law strictly limits the amount you can set aside. You can be penalized for making excessive contributions. You can also be hit if you tap any of your Keogh funds prematurely. Unless you die or are severely disabled, these funds cannot be touched until age 59½. You must start drawing benefits by age 70½.

However, there is nothing to stop you from taking your funds from one qualified HR 10 plan and placing them in another, in the event you feel a different approach is warranted. If you do change, though, be sure the new program has been properly established and that funds go directly from one plan to the other. If they pass through your hands, IRS might tap you for a premature distribution.

Several investment avenues are available. (1) You can join a qualified bank trust, which might include pooled pension funds of a professional or business group, or an individual qualified bank custodial account can be set up. (2) You can take out a qualified annuity plan with an insurance company. (3) You can invest in mutual funds, but the shares must be held by a bank or trust company as custodian. (4) You can purchase special nonmarketable Treasury retirement bonds (hardly suitable in these inflationary days). (5) You can purchase IRS-approved face-amount certificates (a form of annuity).

To make it easier and less expensive for you to begin a Keogh program, "master plans" and "prototype plans" have evolved. Under a master plan, several individual plans are grouped together, funded, and administered in common by a bank or insurance company. A prototype plan is individually administered under sponsorship of a professional association or a regulated investment company. If you are joining a master or prototype plan or will use U.S. bonds, you need only submit a single form to IRS. If you decide to start your own administered plan, you will have to spell it out more completely.

NEWEST WRINKLE: IRA'S

The 1974 law that liberalized HR 10 ceilings also created a new retirement savings vehicle for workers who are not self-employed. Individual retirement accounts, popularly known as IRAs, have had a far more enthusiastic reception than Keogh plans did back in 1962. Patterned after Keogh plans, they allow individuals to shelter up to 15% of their earned income to a $1,500 annual total. However, to be eligible, workers may not be active participants in any qualified pension program. Moves already are afoot in

Congress both to raise the ceilings and to broaden the eligibility requirements.

"SHOULD I INCORPORATE MY PRACTICE?"

Ever since the tax laws gave corporations more generous opportunities than individuals for sheltering retirement funds, professionals like doctors, dentists, lawyers, and accountants have yearned to incorporate. Until recent years, state laws prohibited formation of professional service corporations, and the Internal Revenue Service also frowned heavily on the idea. But the prohibitions have been successfully challenged in the courts, and IRS has given a grudging okay. Now all states permit at least limited incorporation by such practitioners. Still, IRS watches them like a hawk, so you have to hew to the straight and narrow if you go that route.

If you are among the considerable number of professionals considering the move, your decision should take into account these points. Some financial advisers counsel against going it alone as a professional corporation lest you invite IRS claims that you are a personal holding company and thus subject your income to a much stiffer tax rate than for corporations. However, others argue that this is no threat as long as the corporation pays out all income to you either as salary or into your pension and/or profit-sharing plan each year. Be sure your attorney has come to grips with this point before proceeding.

On the other hand, if you are contemplating teaming up with others anyway, a corporation is generally regarded as a better alternative than a partnership. One reason is that in a partnership either party can be held liable for debts incurred by the other, while in a corporation liability is limited to the corporation itself. Another is that it is easier to break off a relationship under a corporate structure.

You must also be willing to undertake the considerable expense and detailed financial probing involved in incorporation. One of the reasons it's easier to break off a corporate relationship than a partnership is that most of the details of division of assets are taken care of at the start. But this means considerable negotiating among the corporators as to who will receive how much salary, how the pension and profit-sharing programs will be set up, who will get how much of these, and so on.

Finally, you should be convinced that your income and the amount you expect to be able to sock away warrant the trouble and expense of incorporation. If the amount you can put aside for retirement isn't a great deal more than the maximum amount allowed under Keogh plans—and note the advent of higher Keogh ceilings previously mentioned—perhaps you should think twice about incorporating.

THE "PROS" ARE ATTRACTIVE

These caveats behind, let's look at some of the advantages of incorporation. Although the new pension law takes big steps toward closing the gap between Keogh plans and corporate pension and profit-sharing programs, some disparities remain that favor corporations.

For one thing, corporate plans still enjoy more generous and flexible rules on contributions on behalf of the employee (which a professional becomes in his own corporation). This is particularly so with profit-sharing plans, which escape some of the provisions of the law. In certain instances, up to 25% of an employee's salary can be sheltered under a corporate plan.

In addition, the new law gives corporate plans three alternatives for establishing vesting standards for employees. This means more flexibility than afforded under Keogh, which flatly states that all full-time workers with three or more years of service must be fully vested. Vesting is the guarantee of pension rights after a worker reaches a certain age and/or number of years of service.

Other advantages of a corporate structure include deferred compensation arrangements, tax-free sick pay, tax-deductible life insurance premiums, and tax-free medical expense reimbursement plans.

If you do decide to incorporate, there are ways to ease the

expense; some stockbrokers offer preapproved pension and profit-sharing plans which your corporation can join, avoiding the costs of setting up your own.

Because of the complexity of incorporation and the many tax and other implications, plus the special considerations dictated by the laws of your state, you should take the step only after careful study of your own situation by your attorney and accountant.

25

Are Your Affairs in Order?

As your investment portfolio grows, so too does its relative importance in your family's entire financial planning picture. In the early years of your career and family life, you might be able to get by with a rather casual approach to your "estate." You probably could list most of your assets from memory and number them on the fingers of both hands.

But as time goes on, assets grow, and responsibilities mount, you begin thinking more seriously about keeping track of what you have, and of how to handle the family's wealth in a way that will yield the greatest benefit.

This chapter addresses itself to the task of helping you draft such a system of record keeping. Then it goes briefly into the care and feeding of your stock certificates—the proof of possession of the assets in your portfolio. Finally, it talks in broad terms about how administration of the family wealth should be handled, both while you are alive (if you are the principal breadwinner) and after you're gone.

KEEPING THINGS STRAIGHT

The backbone of any personal financial planning program is a sound system of record keeping. By maintaining one, you'll always be able to tell at a glance where you stand. What's more, your family will have ready access to the information they need if and when you are not there to tell them where it is.

Agreed, you say. Where do I begin? A good place to start is to decide what information should be gathered, then to pull it all together into one place. One man who has done it has this basic collection of data in a loose-leaf binder:

Will—Note where copies are filed, when it was last drawn, and when any changes were made.

Safe-Deposit Boxes—Note where they are located and list their contents as of a certain date.

Insurance—List all policies and their numbers, and note where they are located and whom to contact if needed.

Bank Accounts—Note account numbers, location of passbooks, and other pertinent information on all family accounts.

Securities—Provide a complete current listing, including costs, and note where certificates are located.

Real Estate—Maintain a list of capital improvements with supporting invoices for tax purposes; note basic expenses such as property taxes, utilities, etc., as well as mortgage data.

Income Taxes—File final returns for the past twenty years and keep complete data for the current year and the preceding six years.

Requests and Recommendations—Provide notes on disposition of personal effects, etc., after death for sentimental or other reasons not specifically mentioned in the will, provide suggestions for surviving spouse as to how he or she might obtain fullest benefit from available resources, and list obituary material.

Professional Advisers—List names of attorney, trustee, and executor of the estate, insurance agents, stockbrokers, and tax counsel.

Once your records are assembled, you shouldn't keep them a secret. If you are a married man, go over them with your wife, explaining each item and its significance. Preferably, she should play an important part in the day-to-day execution of your financial program so she will not be a stranger to it if suddenly it is thrust upon her to shoulder alone. Many a widow without this experience in a very short time goes through the estate it took her husband a working lifetime to accumulate. Then she is left without the financial security he thought he had provided.

But contemplation of death shouldn't be the only motivating force behind establishing a good record-keeping system. If you sell your house, it can help you establish costs so you can reduce any capital gains tax liability on appreciated value. If the IRS challenges your tax return, you can have your defense readily at hand. You can tell at a glance how your investment portfolio is performing.

The earlier you start such a system the more help it can be to you in preserving your hard-earned assets and making them work more efficiently for you.

SAFEGUARDING YOUR SECURITIES

Here, in descending order, are our recommendations as to how your stock certificates should be held:

1. Obtain and safeguard them yourself. You may execute transfers directly if you sell, and you will have immediate access if you need them for such things as loan collateral. The best bet, of course, is your safe-deposit box at the bank.

2. Place them in your own name and deposit with a bank or with your attorney. If you must be away from home for extended periods, you may sell shares by signing a stock power and sending it to the custodian. Or you may assign power of attorney beforehand.

3. Place them in your own name and keep them on deposit with your broker. Sale can be executed with a signed stock power.

But back-office logjams can result in delays in obtaining certificates. Lost certificates are not rarities, either.

4. Keep them in "street name." This means leaving your certificates in your broker's name, in his possession, for you. This is the least desirable alternative, though for frequent traders clearly the most convenient. But besides running the risk of lost or mislaid certificates, you have no direct control over them. This means, for example, that your broker can lend your certificates to someone else who wishes to sell short! Such short sellers sometimes do get in trouble! So do brokers themselves. Think of all those who went broke in the 1969–73 years. Thus, even with the Securities Investor Protection Act that insures against such losses, your investment could be tied up for a long time if something goes wrong.

IF YOUR BROKER GOES BROKE . . .

The Securities Investor Protection Act of 1970 created the Securities Investor Protection Corporation, a federally backed insurance program funded by mandatory contributions from brokerage firms with the government ready to step in if liquidations exhaust the kitty. Each investor is protected up to a $50,000 total, including a maximum $20,000 in cash.

The SIPC received its first big test in the spring of 1973 when it was forced to handle the liquidation of Weis Securities, Inc., a major brokerage firm. Previously, it had presided—smoothly, for the most part—over the close of four-score small houses.

A brief look at the Weis situation will give you an idea of how SIPC works, to both the advantage and the disadvantage of investors.

In the Weis liquidation, one major complaint was that stock certificates were not immediately returned to customers. This was because much of the stock was being held by banks as collateral against some $40 million in loans outstanding. Weis, in turn, had lent the funds to its margin accounts. The banks had sold much of the stock in a declining market to protect their assets.

As a result, there were not enough shares to go around when

they were distributed to Weis customers. Furthermore, cash restitution for the absent stock was made on the basis of per-share
valuations as of May 24. Since this was just before a sizable
market rally, some customers were dealt substantial losses.

Nevertheless, the liquidation was achieved with relative speed.
As of mid-October, 98% of the customer claims had been paid off,
with only a minimal number generating objections. Of the $35.1
million distributed, $16.3 million came from SIPC. Thus, without
the insurance program, Weis customers certainly would have
received much less than they did.

Despite the speed with which SIPC attended to the liquidation
and the amount of its own funds provided to make up losses, the
experience provides one more example of the wisdom, in general,
of obtaining and safeguarding your own stock certificates.

IF YOU LOSE A STOCK CERTIFICATE . . .

If you lose a stock certificate, you can obtain a new one. But
replacement can be a long and costly process. Should it happen to
you, here is what to do.

First, contact the transfer agent of the company involved. The
agent, usually a bank, will place a "stop" on the certificate to bar
its resale. If you have not noted the agent's name, you can find
out through a direct call to the company.

After the certificate has been stopped, you must furnish the
company with a perpetual indemnity bond. This will protect the
firm against any losses it might incur through a reissue. Cost of
the bond will probably be about 4% of the certificate's current
value.

Then, you will have to meet certain conditions established by
the company, and they vary in strictness from firm to firm. No
corporation likes to reissue, and some do their best to discourage
replacement until absolutely sure the security is lost.

At any rate, you should take one more look before buying the
indemnity bond because if you do find the certificate later, you
will get only part of the premium back; after a year, you will get
nothing back.

Prevention, obviously, is the best cure. Take time to be certain your stocks are properly safeguarded.

JOINT OWNERSHIP: BEWARE OF TRAPS

When Mr. and Mrs. A were married, they didn't have much in the way of material things. But over the years, Mr. A worked hard and became a successful businessman. Mrs. A was careful with the family resources. They saved regularly and invested wisely. Devoted to one another, they held dearly to the time-honored concept that "what's mine is yours, what's yours is mine."

They placed everything in joint names with right of survivorship. The house. Bank accounts. Stock certificates. Savings bonds. The business. Other real estate. When one died, the property—all of it—would pass directly to the other. Their wills left everything to be equally divided among the children afterward. The ultimate in simplicity. But potentially the arrangement could prove extremely and unnecessarily expensive.

A big reason is estate taxes. A common fallacy holds that half of jointly owned property automatically belongs to each party. Not so. If Mr. A contributed all of it to the kitty, all of it is counted to his estate if he dies first. In fact, unless Mrs. A can *prove* any contribution, it would be presumed that Mr. A had contributed it all.

Under the marital deduction, half of Mr. A's estate would be exempted from the death tax. But on Mrs. A's subsequent death, with no marital deduction to ease the bite, the entire estate (less taxes and administrative costs of probating it after Mr. A's death) is taxed again. The effect is to tax the assets of Mr. and Mrs. A one and a half times, if one of them outlives the other by ten years or more. (If one dies within ten years after the death of the other, the estate of the survivor is allowed a credit depending on the length of time elapsed.)

By careful division of their property while they are alive, by careful drawing of wills, and perhaps by establishment of trusts, it may be possible to reduce estate taxes very substantially.

ESTATE PLANNING RESTRICTED

Another disadvantage of joint ownership is a loss of control in estate planning. Under joint ownership with right of survivorship, one of the owners cannot spell out in a will conditions under which his "share" of the property can be distributed. It all goes to the other party automatically. Thus, Mr. A would not be able to specify conditions, say, under which one son would run the business, the other administer the real estate interests.

Gift taxes while the As are alive pose another potential problem under joint ownership. Since Mr. A is contributing all of the assets, he is, in effect, making "gifts" to his wife. Two factors determine the value of the gifts. One is the value at the time the property is placed in joint names; the other is the extent of interest in the property the noncontributing owner acquires at the time. In some states it is half; in others it is determined using a formula based on age of each owner and government mortality tables.

Many couples, ignorant of this gift tax obligation, suddenly find themselves faced not only with gift taxes themselves, but with penalties involved for failure to declare them.

Naturally, no gift is involved in property in which both contribute to the price in the same proportion as their individual interest. Neither is a gift involved in a joint bank account—unless the noncontributing owner withdraws funds for his own use. The same is true of U.S. Savings Bonds, where no gift tax obligation results unless the noncontributing owner cashes in the bonds. Finally, no gift is considered in joint purchase by husband and wife of a home or other real estate unless the property is later sold and proceeds divided disproportionately to each partner's actual contribution.

THERE ARE ALTERNATIVES

When Mr. and Mrs. A realized the estate planning traps they had set, they understandably wanted to unspring them. What should they do?

First, it isn't such a bad idea to keep the house in joint names. That way, the widow acquires it at once when her husband dies. The same for a bank account with enough money in it to carry her over the first rough months until the estate is settled.

They could decide to divide all other property equally, including securities and other real estate, by changing from joint tenancy to tenancy in common, dropping the right of survivorship. This way, each can dispose of his share via a will. Any gift tax liability of the husband should be far less than the reduction of estate taxes which would be accomplished. If the situation of the fictional Mr. and Mrs. A sounds a lot like your own, you might want to think seriously about sitting down with your attorney and doing some comprehensive estate planning.

CHOOSING AN EXECUTOR

If you're the well-ordered type, with your financial affairs up to snuff, you've probably given considerable thought to the possibility that your family might be required to carry on in your absence. To that end, you have assessed their probable needs and drawn up a will with those needs clearly in mind.

Well and good. But have you given comparably careful consideration to the choice of an executor of your estate? Too often a hasty decision in this regard ultimately undoes much of a person's otherwise careful planning and estate-building efforts.

IS WIFE A LOGICAL CHOICE?

Many men, understandably, designate their wife as executrix. There is considerable logic to the choice. After all, she is the closest to the situation, and knows better than anyone else what your family's needs are, what your aspirations are, what you would want done.

But there is always the nagging possibility that she might not possess the financial and managerial sophistication to watch over the estate properly or to preserve its assets adequately. This will be increasingly so as she advances in years.

The same could be said for a son or daughter, brother or close family friend. These, too, are frequently named executors. Even the family lawyer, another seemingly logical choice, might lack the expertise necessary to manage your affairs effectively.

On the other hand, an attorney specializing in estate management or a bank or trust company might not be as close to the family situation as a friend or relative, and might make decisions quite alien to your own desires or, possibly, to the real needs of the family.

An executor's task is not one to be taken lightly. In a small estate, with no major complications, where the will's intentions are clearly spelled out and there is not much property to dispose of or heirs to offer dispute, the job can be relatively easy. But in an estate of any substance, where there are children or an elderly widow and their continuing financial security to consider, or where family quarrels erupt, the job can be far from routine.

CHANGING EXECUTORS IS COSTLY

In such cases, the availability of an executor could be required over the span of several years. Can you be sure the person of your choice would meet this test? He could die or move away or be otherwise unable to carry on. In this event, a new executor would have to be appointed, at considerable expense to the estate. Unless you had designated someone as an alternative choice, a court-appointed replacement might handle the estate at a variance with your wishes.

Furthermore, an executor should have experience in this type of work. He should have the ability to conserve the estate's assets and administer them prudently. He should be financially responsible.

To be sure, an executor can be held legally responsible for the estate's assets if he carelessly handles them, say, by losing money on speculative investments or by illegally diverting them. He can be held liable for actions he has failed to take with regard to the estate as well, such as failure to pay taxes, bills, or other obligations resulting in losses.

However, if the executor is not able to make restitution for such drains on the assets, the heirs would be the ultimate losers. To prevent such losses, many wills specify that the executor be bonded. The cost of insurance bond premiums comes out of the estate, but it is a worthwhile expense, even if the executor is a close friend or family member.

CONSIDER CO-EXECUTORS

You would not face such problems with an institutional executor, since the courts regard them as financially responsible, and they do not "die." However, if you do decide to use an institution as executor you should exercise care in the choice. As in other things, there is a difference in quality of service between one institution and another. Your family lawyer can help you decide.

If you are able to get to know the people at your bank on a personal basis, you could name the bank as executor with confidence that it would carry out your wishes. But if you don't have this confidence, perhaps you could consider naming your wife and the bank as co-executors. Carrying this one step further, you could give your wife the final say in any decision. Thus, she would provide the continuity in your family's life-style, while the professional executor would provide the good management, attend to the details, and be available to offer expert counsel.

You are in the best position to know who will serve your family's interests well in your stead, if that ever becomes necessary. But you should make the choice only after considerable thought and possibly some advice from professionals. Your decision can be as important as the care you take in preparing your will.

26

Taxes and Your Investments

Tax laws change, often from year to year, so it is difficult to be definitive in giving tax instructions in a book like this. It's much better for you to go to your own tax experts when the time for paying taxes is reasonably in sight.

Further, you should never let tax considerations dictate investment policy. Don't sell a good stock you hold at a loss just because you can use the loss for tax purposes. The stock you sell may come back faster than the one you buy to replace it. You don't sell a good stock just for the sake of taking a profit, either.

"Cut your losses and let your profits run" is a hoary old Wall Street saying. So also is its counterpart, "You'll never go broke taking profits." Both miss the point. If a stock is attractive, hold onto it, whether it shows a profit or a loss at the moment. Conversely, if it's unattractive, sell it and use the money to buy something with more appeal.

TAX LOSSES CAN HELP

Having delivered such eminently sensible advice, let's backtrack enough to demonstrate that selling for tax purposes sometimes can reduce your tax liability without injuring your investment position. Let's suppose you bought 100 shares of a good electric utility such as Arizona Public Service at 28, only to see rising interest rates and rampant inflation depress the entire electric utility group until your stock is down to 18. Your loss is $1,000.

If you held the stock for six months or less, you can use all of the $1,000 loss as an offset against your ordinary income. In other words, if you sell your Arizona Public Service and subtract the resulting loss from your ordinary income you will save in taxes (and thus recoup in losses) only to the extent that your tax bracket bears on $1,000. Thus, if you are in a 35% bracket, your tax bill will be $350 lower, if you are in a 40% bracket, $400 lower, and so on. If you held the stock for more than six months, only half of the loss can be used to offset ordinary income.*

Either way, short or long term, losses offer savings worth considering. On the other hand, it's tough to sell a good stock when it's down. If your Arizona Public Service should come back to your cost, you would be recouping the whole $1,000, not just $350 or $400. One way you can protect yourself against such a recovery is to reinvest the sale proceeds in another good electric utility, such as Atlantic City Electric.

Note the charts on pages 228–29 of these two companies. They almost always move together. Thus, it is realistic to expect to sell one and buy the other (giving yourself a tax saving by taking a capital loss) without really losing your investment position.

The same thing can be done with two international oils (Texaco and Mobil), two drugs (Pfizer and Warner-Lambert), or two coal stocks (Eastern Gas & Fuel and Westmoreland). But be careful. The less similar the two issues are, the more you run the risk of seeing the stock you sell recover while the stock you buy sinks.

Taking losses to offset other income is one thing. Taking losses to offset profits taken is a "must." It is patently ridiculous, for example, to sell Levitz Furniture because of a terrific run-up in price to what you consider unsupportable levels, and pay a

---

* As this is written, there are moves afoot in Congress to change the tax rules on capital gains and losses. Be sure to take into account any such changes as you consider the tax implications of your portfolio.

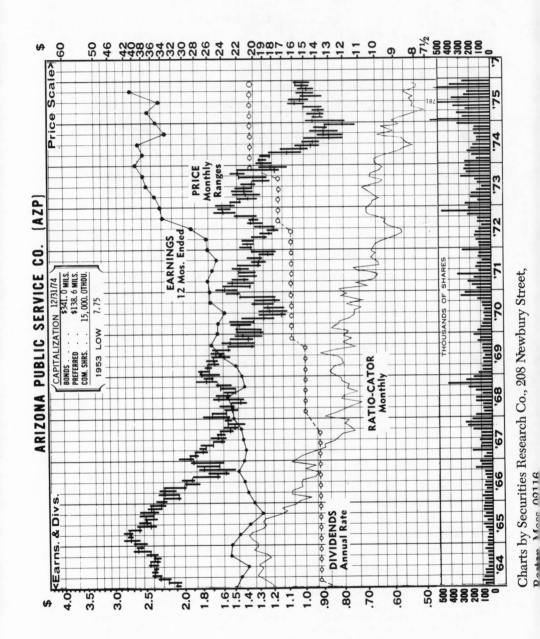

ARIZONA PUBLIC SERVICE CO. (AZP)

Charts by Securities Research Co., 208 Newbury Street,
Boston, Mass. 02116

ATLANTIC CITY ELECTRIC CO. [ATE]

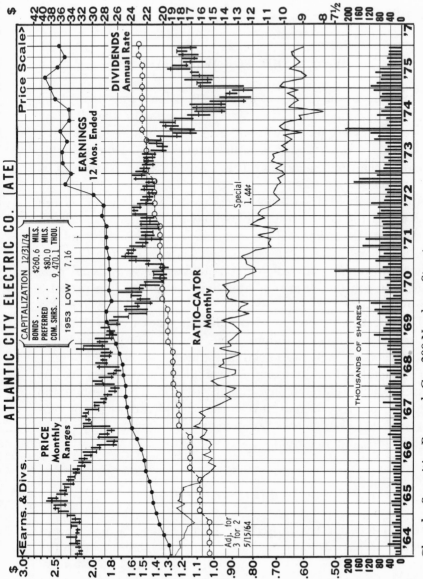

Price Scale▶

PRICE
Monthly
Ranges

EARNINGS
12 Mos. Ended

DIVIDENDS
Annual Rate

RATIO-CATOR
Monthly

CAPITALIZATION 12/31/74

BONDS	$260.6	MILS.
PREFERRED	$80.0	MILS.
COM. SHRS. . .	9,470.1	THOU.

1953 LOW   7.16

Special
1.44¢

Adj. for
3 for 2
5/15/64

THOUSANDS OF SHARES

Chart by Securities Research Co., 208 Newbury Street,
Boston, Mass. 02116

capital gains tax, when you have equivalent unrealized losses in other holdings. Whenever possible, then, balance profits taken on sales made for investment reasons with losses you have "on paper."

WATCH OUT FOR WASH SALES

It is possible to sell a stock to register a loss for tax purposes, then buy the same stock back. But you must keep more than 30 days between transactions. (If you buy back sooner you've registered a "wash sale," which under tax rules prevents you from claiming the loss.) This means more of a risk. Anything can happen in 30 days on the stock market.

Another way to skin this particular cat is to "double up." If you wish to sell 100 GM to record a loss, buy an additional 100 shares of the stock first, *then* sell the original. Again, you must not sell the old shares before at least 30 days elapse from the time the new ones were bought, lest you run afoul of the "wash sale" rule. Thus, you can double up no later than December 1 to record a loss in that year.

The safest thing to do is to switch from stock in one company to stock in a completely different one, simultaneously recording a loss and getting back into a good investment.

The moral of this discussion is twofold. First, don't let tax loss considerations rule your investment program. That's letting the tail wag the dog. Second, investment considerations being central, real dollars-and-cents tax savings can be made if you keep good records and do it right.

A WORD ON PROFITS

Many an investor has missed the boat because he or she was reluctant to pay capital gains taxes. Probably more opportunities have been lost this way than any other. If a stock catches the market's favor and soars to unreasonable heights, sell it. Let someone else have it. Take your profit. Give Uncle Sam his share and count your blessings.

As an example, consider the bowling fad of the late 1950s and early 1960s. This all started with the development of the automatic pinsetter which freed bowling alleys of a terrific labor problem. No one wanted to be a pinboy. The poor fellow was a latter-day Sisyphus. The faster he set up the pins, the quicker they were knocked down. He could get nowhere.

Pinboys, therefore, were hard to come by, and expensive. The automatic pinsetter changed all that. No more pinboys, no more labor trouble, and lower costs. Bowling alley construction boomed. Pinsetter makers and bowling alley builders prospered and their shares soared. By early 1961 AMF had shot up to prices over 60, and was selling at 41 times earnings. Three years earlier it sold at a price of 12 and a more reasonable P/E of 15.

Then came the disillusion. Soon there seemed to be more alleys than bowlers, and earnings tapered off. AMF plunged to 18 in 1962, then settled into a range nearer its normal 15 times earnings. The rise and fall of Brunswick was even more spectacular— from less than 1 to 70 and back to 10. In both cases it was obvious that the boom was absurd and couldn't last. What did the stockholders of these two companies expect, a bowling alley on every corner? Nothing less would have supported the top prices of these shares.

Yet, how many holders refused to let go because of capital gains taxes? Plenty.

GIFTS AND TAXES

So much for income tax implications of the gains and losses you score on your investments. Suppose you have enjoyed many more gains than losses over the years, and the time has come to consider giving away some of your good fortune. Uncle Sam is looking over your shoulder here, too, waiting to get his cut of the gift or estate taxes due him.

As matters stand at the time of this writing, old Uncle regards it more blessed to give while you're alive than after you're gone. At least, he taxes you less for the former. Tax "reformers" have long sought to equalize the disparity in gift and estate tax provisions that rather generously favor gifts, and some tightening could well come soon. But until it does—if it hasn't by the time you read this—the following comments might help you to take advantage of existing tax benefits.

GIFTS TO INDIVIDUALS

Under present law, you can give up to $3,000 per person to any number of individuals each year before you are subject to gift taxes. In addition, you have a one-time $30,000 lifetime exclusion to be used as you see fit. (The limits are $6,000 and $60,000 respectively for a married couple.) Furthermore, gifts you make to your spouse can be calculated at half their value, provided they are not considered community property.

Gifts made to individuals are not deductible against your income tax. Recipients are not liable for taxes on gifts given them, but they must pay taxes on income generated by the gifts.

Many parents use gifts to their children as a means of reducing tax liability on income earned by these gifts, since the children probably would be taxed in a lower bracket.

If you elect to shift income from securities in this way, you must be sure to register the securities in the name of a custodian on behalf of the child, if he is a minor. The custodian retains management powers over the securities and the child assumes possession on reaching majority.

As long as the income from the custodian account is not used for the child's support, IRS regards it as a tax obligation of the child. You might be wise to appoint someone other than yourself as custodian; otherwise if you die before the child attains majority, the gift might be included in your taxable estate. Also, if you list yourself as custodian, IRS might not regard the transfer as a gift, but as a "future interest" (see later discussion).

A new point to consider in making gifts to minors is the trend in more states toward lowering the age of majority. If your state is one of these, this could mean assets would go to the child at age 18 instead of 21. You might regard this as too young. On the other hand, if the assets do pass to him at a lower age, their use to pay college expenses and support could mean big income tax savings for you.

CHARITABLE CONTRIBUTIONS

A gift to a domestic nonprofit organization of a religious, charitable, scientific, literary, or educational nature which is qualified is deductible from federal income taxes. It is not subject to gift taxes, either.

Deductions for gifts to organized charities are restricted generally to 50% of adjusted gross income. In the case of appreciated property which if sold would have brought long-term capital gain (held over six months) you can deduct the market value, under a 30% of gross income ceiling, though you can elect instead to use the 50% ceiling if you reduce the amount of deduction by one half of the gain you would have realized by selling the property. In the case of appreciated property which if sold would have brought ordinary income, deduction is limited to your cost, rather than market value.

If you wish to sell appreciated long-term capital gain property to a charitable organization for your cost, your deduction is limited to the gain on the sale. You must also report as capital gain the portion of sale proceeds attributed to your cost.

Careful planning can increase the value of your gifts and reduce both your gift tax and income tax liability. But since certain limitations might apply to your own case, we suggest you consult your tax adviser before making any definite commitments.

POINTS TO REMEMBER

Future Interests—If you make gifts that are not present interests, such as retaining the right to name beneficiaries or to allocate income from the property, the gift is regarded as a future interest and cannot be protected by the annual exclusion.

Losses—If you wish to give securities on which you have a loss, sell them first to establish the loss, then donate the proceeds. You may deduct the gift of the proceeds and claim the loss on the sale.

Timing—A charitable gift is deductible in the year received, so you should be sure the transfer is completed on or before December 31 for deduction on that year's return. On securities, the gift is considered completed (1) on delivery of the properly endorsed certificate directly to the donee or his agent or (2) on the date the stock is transferred on the corporation's books if the certificate is delivered to your bank or broker for forwarding to the recipient.

27

Where Do I Get Advice?

One of the questions I am asked most frequently as I travel about the country speaking to investors is a desperately uttered, "Where can I get honest-to-goodness advice?"

This is a tough question to answer for a number of reasons. First, the asker often expects more from his adviser than probably is humanly possible to deliver. The engineer often expects the investment world to be as finite and logical as his. Physicians who know that medicine regularly misses on a predictable percentage of diagnoses rarely give the investment professional the same leeway. Otherwise gentle and loving mothers become veritable tigresses when their savings shrink as the market goes against them. Only the experienced and thoughtful investor knows and accepts the frailties of any investment adviser—be he banker, broker, counselor, or financial writer.

EXPERIENCE HELPS

So also is the intelligent investor better able to get good advice. He has been around long enough to know the superficial, appreciate the possible, and recognize the charlatan. The answer to the question, "Where do I get advice?" is, therefore: "In a number of places."

First, your broker can give you good information and advice if he has a good office to back him up. Rare is the one-man office that can really deliver on this score; but a brokerage office with access to real research can be a big help. But remember that your broker survives only on commissions. Thus, he is eternally pressured to advise change, for transactions mean income for him.

Speaking of brokers, we might mention here a new phenomenon in the industry—the "unbundled" broker. This all started with the determination of the SEC to open brokerage commissions to the brisk wind of unfettered competition. For all of history, the charges for buying and selling stocks have been fixed. All brokers were forced to charge the same rates for buying and selling securities. The business was "fair-traded."

For good reason the SEC considered such fixed prices anomalous in a free-enterprise society, particularly for the brokerage business which was theoretically, and certainly philosophically, as close to the center of that free-enterprise society as one could get. Naturally, the industry objected. Although everyone believes in competition, no one really wants it himself. But the SEC persevered and ruled that the portion of all trades above $500,000 could be negotiated. The limit was then dropped to $300,000. Then, as of April 1, 1974, trades of $2,000 or less were freed. For the vast bulk of trades between these limits, negotiated fees were put off until May 1, 1975. Since then, the brokers have been living in a freely competitive society like the rest of us.

YOU PAYS YOUR MONEY . . .

All of this has produced the "unbundled" broker. This term refers to the separation of the various services offered by a broker, and his charging you only for those services you use. For example, Merrill Lynch offers research, custodianship, and investment advice as well as actual brokerage. Under the old system, you paid for all three whether you used them or not.

Under the newly developed system, your broker can charge you only for the services you actually use. If all your broker does is execute a purchase or sale for you, your cost should be modest. If you ask for advice and counsel too, you must pay more. If you subscribe to the firm's research output or request custodial arrangements for your stock certificates, you will pay more again.

. . . AND TAKES YOUR CHOICE

Naturally, this new concept for the brokerage business has immediately spawned a few firms that do buying and selling only. They are, in effect, "discount" brokers. They could be all right for you, too. Just be sure your discount broker is on solid financial ground. Ask your local bank and find out from other customers if routine services are efficient. For example, do they deliver certificates with reasonable speed?

As for brokerage costs generally, we do not expect much of a decline, even with free competition. Costs are just too high. Inflation affects this industry as much as it does the rest of us.

Another source of advice is your bank. Bankers offer counsel to investors through their trust departments. Quality varies, depending on size, staff skills, and, too often, the size of your account. Trust departments must live, too, so this advice also usually involves a fee. Here again, a discerning eye on the part of the investor will go a long way in separating the wheat from the chaff. Of course, that's always easier said than done. It's often hard to actually get a look at performance when it comes to banks.

Here's the experience of a group of leading banks, the places where the canniest money men are supposed to be, for the three years 1971–73. This is what they were able to do with the funds entrusted to them for investment.

The figures show what you know already: that no one, not even

Bank	1971	1972	1973	3 Years 1971–73°
Bank of New York	+19.5%	+19.7%	−11.2%	+8.3%
Bankers Trust	+25.1%	+20.5%	−28.4%	+2.5%
Chase Manhattan	+15.1%	+6.5%	−17.9%	+0.2%
Chemical Bank	+25.9%	+11.4%	−16.3%	+5.5%
Citibank	+22.8%	+22.4%	−18.3%	+7.1%
Irving Trust	+18.1%	+22.5%	−18.4%	+5.9%
Manufacturers Hanover	+22.8%	+25.1%	−20.2%	+7.0%
Morgan Guaranty	+18.1%	+25.9%	−20.8%	+5.6%
U.S. Trust	+28.4%	+21.9%	−22.9%	+6.5%
Bank Average	+21.9%	+19.5%	−19.1%	+5.4%
S&P 425 Industrials	+15.0%	+20.1%	−14.9%	+5.5%

° Average growth compounded annually.

New York's mightiest banks, has a corner on investment acumen —or good luck, either. But these have been tough years for investors, big and little alike. History shows that such stock market "storms" always end, and when they do, stock prices catch up in a rush. The big banks know this. That's why they hang on. As we have preached, *ad nauseam* perhaps, elsewhere in this treatise, individual investors should do the same.

LEAVE THE "DRIVING" TO US

Finally, in our list of sources of investment advice (and we list these not in their order of preference), we include investment counselors. They come in two sizes, big and little. Big ones generally will not handle accounts much under $300,000. When they do take your account they provide investment advice in depth. The initiative is theirs. They watch your portfolio constantly and carefully, notifying you when they believe changes should be made. Although they are always glad to answer any questions you may have and consider any suggestions you offer, they carry the main responsibility for the health of your account on their own shoulders. Under this arrangement you don't have to do any thinking yourself. This sort of service costs, too, but usually only a modest one half of 1%, or less, annually of the actual amount under supervision. (It should come as no surprise to readers that

United Business Service offers just such a service through its wholly-owned subsidiary, United Investment Counsel.)

Then there are the mini-counselors who offer similar advice for those with as little as $20,000–$25,000. Because of the small size of the accounts and the need to computerize, this type of account is almost always discretionary. Where the owner of the big account usually holds his own certificates and uninvested cash, retains and instructs his own broker (after agreeing or disagreeing with the advice he gets), the mini-counsel client puts everything in the hands of the counsel firm—stock certificates, cash, and investment decisions alike.

If there is a transaction he doesn't like, he cannot say no as the larger client can, for it will be a *fait accompli* before he's even privy to it. The mini-account is also expensive to handle, so the fees are much larger. They often start at 2% annually, scaling down as size goes up.

Then there are published investment advisers for investors who don't want to pay for investment counsel and think that brokers are too commission-oriented. These range from large, old-time industry leaders such as Standard & Poor's, Value Line Survey, and, of course, United Business Service, to one-man, one-type-writer, one-page fliers.

The big ones all attempt to give investors a realistic view of the stock and bond markets with specific suggestions of securities to buy or sell. All are based on the fundamentals of assets, earnings, and dividends. None are based on astrology, cycles, or charts. Charts are an important tool in the so-called technical approach. The technician assumes that the very track of the market or of an individual stock will, when charted, predict its future performance. To this, of course, you should say, "Phooey." Fundamentals are all there are to go by.

HOW CAN YOU RATE THE ADVISERS?

Once you have found a source of advice, how do you determine how good it has been for you? This is easy. Just total your portfolio at regular intervals and compare its expansions and contractions with that of the Dow-Jones Industrial Average, or with any other of the well-known averages that appeals to you.

Recognize that if you have a growth-accentuated stock list you should be doing better than the Dow, and if your principal flavor is income you will probably be lagging. If you have any questions, just show your comparison to your adviser and see what he says. As long as your account is moving along with the market, or a little better, you'll be doing okay. Your savings dollars will be doubling about every eight years—and that is nothing to sniff at.

Unless you have all the time in the world, it's pretty hard to apply the do-it-yourself approach to investment advice. Not that you couldn't master the techniques; anyone with a reasonably logical mind could learn to apply the various "tests" to potential investments and to size one up against others. But, to do it well takes time, and that's a commodity most of us find in short supply.

READ THE ANNUAL REPORTS

There is one thing you can do, though, that might add a bit of insight to your understanding of the companies in which you hold stocks. That is to pay closer attention to their annual reports. If you've only been looking at the photographs in these publications, you're not getting half the picture. The text can tell you a lot about the companies—if you read it right.

Of course, unless you're a financial analyst much of the information won't be too meaningful. But with a little guidance, a lot of it can be.

Let's take it from the top. Statements by the president, chairman, or both, will tell you where the company has been, where it hopes to go, what contributed to its success, what held it back. More than likely, these reports will have a rose-colored tint. But they'll be accurate—there are strict regulatory and stock exchange provisions to assure this. From these messages you might be able to tell where the company hopes to expand and perhaps get some idea of management's sales and earnings expectations.

So far, so good. It's not the prose that turns off most annual report readers, it's the figures and footnotes. But this is where the real nuggets are mined—in the balance sheet and the operating statement.

The balance sheet has been compared with a medical report—it is a picture of the company's financial health on the last day of its business year. It balances the company's assets against its liabilities and stockholders' equity.

The operating statement, also frequently called the profit-and-loss statement or the earnings statement, reviews the company's progress over the past year. At the top will be figures for total revenues generated by sales of the company's goods or services. Costs of producing these goods or services are subtracted, leaving gross profit. From this, operating expenses, depreciation, interest charges, and other costs are deducted, leaving pretax operating profit. Finally, taxes are subtracted, yielding the most eagerly sought figure: net earnings.

Often, too, the annual report will contain a comparison of figures for the past five or ten years. These can give you some insights as to the direction in which the company is heading.

In your examination of the report, don't overlook the footnotes. They can contain another wealth of information, such as descriptions of intercompany transactions, explanations of depreciation methods, or details about accounting methods used.

Every annual report is rounded out with an auditor's certification, usually accompanied by an opinion that the financial statements present fairly the company's financial position. If the opinion is omitted or is present with disclaimers, this does not necessarily mean the figures are inaccurate or in doubt, but can mean the auditors were unable to verify them for some technical reason.

A HARVEST OF CLUES

What do you do with all these facts? By applying some arithmetic to be detailed here, you can come up with a variety of clues to how the company is doing and, more important, how well it might be expected to do. By comparing data for companies in the same industry you can get an idea of how each is performing.

This broad-brush approach can only touch the highlights of annual report analysis. But in helping you better understand the complex subject, it can also give you some insights into one of the many resources most analysts utilize.

DO SOME ARITHMETIC

Price-Earnings Ratio—Divide price per share by earnings per share. This multiple measures, among other things, investor regard for the stock. The higher the multiple, the greater the popularity. It is useful in comparing one company against others in the same industry.

Stock Yield—Divide the annual dividend per share of stock by the stock price. A higher yield generally is desired for "income" portfolios, while a lower return generally accompanies a "growth" stock. An extremely high yield could be a sign that dividend coverage is shaky and a cut is imminent.

Sales-Inventories Ratio—Divide sales by year-end inventories to obtain inventory turnover. Turnover for some industries is higher than for others, but a generally high turnover usually is an indication of solid demand and a favorable pricing schedule.

Working Capital Ratio—Divide current assets (cash, readily marketable securities, accounts receivable, inventories, etc.) by current liabilities (payable within a year). As a general rule, current assets of at least twice current liabilities are regarded as healthy.

Pretax Profit Margin—Divide sales into operating profit. Because certain costs are fixed, a spurt in sales will help widen the margin.

Liquidity Ratio—Divide current liabilities into cash and readily marketable securities. This indicates the company's ability to meet current debt.

Return on Equity—Divide net income by the sum of the common stock, preferred stock, and surplus accounts. This percentage indicates the earnings which the stockholders' investment produces. The higher the ratio the better.

SECTION FIVE

Investments, Economics, and Politics

THE BACK YARD

One of the many things that have mystified me over the years is the incredible staying power of economists whether they are right, wrong, or indifferent. Consider as a for instance William Simon and Herbert Stein, the two economic luminaries of this Administration.

Whether you are a Republican, Democrat, or Independent you have to admit that they get the brass ring when it comes to the delivery of economic thrills and chills. Under their advice we've had laissez faire, then rigid Government controls. We've had record unemployment, inflation, and interest rates. The dollar has been devalued twice, and our wheat market was very nearly cornered by the Russians.

And yet they stay in power. Think of others in the inner circle who erred far less yet are long gone—Hickel, Finch, Peterson, etc. To show that my observations may be neither specious nor spurious, consider this comment by John Kenneth Galbraith, who is one of the faith.

"Then there is the remarkable non-accountability of economists—something of which, as an economist, I am very reluctant to complain. A surgeon, in a general way, is held accountable for results. If, delving for a brain tumor, he gets a prostate, he is open to criticism. Even lawyers are held to certain standards of performance: John Mitchell is in trouble for changing sides on the matter of crime. But not economists. No matter how great the disaster, we are still revered."

So off we go with Stein and Simon into the umpteenth economic game plan in recent years. Let's keep our fingers crossed.

SEPTEMBER 17, 1973

28

Why It Costs More to Live

For most of us inflation is easy to define. It's just higher prices for the things we buy. But it's also higher prices for the things we sell. Although few of us think of it that way, a cost-of-living adjustment in our salaries, for example, is as much evidence of inflation as an increase in the price of steak.

Higher interest rates are evidence of inflation, too. Interest rates are merely the price of money, and money prices go up with everything else in inflationary periods. Inflation, then, is higher prices for everything. While some items may rise in price faster than others, just about everything does cost more after the country has gone through a bout with inflation.

WHO DUNNIT?

While inflation is easy to define, it is not so easy to see why it happens. Generally speaking, at least as economists generally speak, there are two main kinds of inflation. One is demand-pull, or too many dollars chasing too few things. The other is cost-push, or the steady upward pressure exerted on prices by rising costs.

The best illustration of demand-pull inflation is in a wartime situation when almost everyone goes to work, unemployment falls, and fat paychecks are the weekly reward for our efforts. At the same time, because of the demands of war, little is produced for the civilian economy. During World War II, for example, the tremendous military needs for tanks, ships, guns, and aircraft meant there was no material left over to make autos, radios, refrigerators, or washing machines for the civilian economy. The military had first call on cotton and wool for uniforms, leather for army boots, and, worst of all, it took all of milady's nylon for parachutes.

WARS WILL DO IT . . .

Since people could not spend their money on these things, they chased others. Of course, they saved more than usual, but by and large they sent their excess dollars after what few consumer goods were available. The result was a surge in prices despite an elaborate system of price controls. This was a classic case of demand-pull inflation—too many dollars chasing too few goods.

Barring an increase in the amount of available goods, there is only one way to cure such inflation. That is to cut down on the excess of dollars. This was tried in two ways during World War II. First, income taxes were boosted sizably. Second, people were encouraged to save. Payroll deduction purchases of U.S. War Bonds were a patriotic must. But even these measures were not sufficiently Draconian to siphon off all of the extra money around; hence, the stubborn uptrend in prices during the war years.

. . . EVERY TIME

What this illustrates is that demand-pull inflation is very difficult to stop because the real remedy, a rigorous tax increase, is not popular, and thus probably politically impossible. That is why President Johnson tried to have butter along with the guns during the height of the Vietnam War years. He knew the war was so unpopular that the public would not pay extra taxes to support it. Thus, once again we had a war-originated surge of demand-pull inflation.

Another demand-pull example has occurred more recently. When the dollar dropped in value in 1971–73, the flood of dollars that went to Europe in the 1940s, 1950s, and 1960s began to flow back in the form of huge purchases of U.S. farm products, among other things. The result was the largest surge in food prices in the memory of American grocery shoppers. Too many dollars chasing too few eggs.

ALWAYS BLAME LABOR . . .

The other principal type of inflation, cost-push, is easier to demonstrate if you start by putting the onus on labor—organized labor, that is. Back in the 1960s, particularly in the latter part of that stormy decade, and in the very early 1970s, the country enjoyed a tremendous building boom. Housing starts ran at record levels, well over two million annually, year after year.

This gave labor a marvelous opportunity to boost wages, which it did. George Meany's plumbers went to town, taking with them plasterers, carpenters, electricians, and others. Construction costs zoomed by a torrid 12% a year, and real estate prices promptly reflected the trend. The surge in wage rates was matched by a (demand-pull here) jump in building material prices. Prices of homes probably rose more in those years, 1968–72, than in any comparable period in our history. That's cost-push.

. . . OR MANAGEMENT

Organized labor does contribute to inflation of the cost-push variety. So does management. In most cities in recent years clerical labor has been short. Company has competed with company to get enough youthful typists, file clerks, messengers, and keypunch operators to keep the mountains of paperwork that is so much a part of our complex society in some sort of order. As these back-office costs soared for the brokerage industry, for example, it eagerly sought and finally obtained better commissions—or higher prices. Again, cost-push inflation.

CONTROLS CAN'T DO IT

Most governments, here and abroad, capitalistic or socialistic, enlightened or repressive, resort to controls in times of inflation. Why? Because the alternatives to price and wage controls as a means of controlling inflation are politically difficult and socially unpleasant.

Why won't controls work? Because they treat the symptom rather than the disease. And they are unfair. Someone is always being squeezed between rising costs and fixed prices. Not only is this unfair to the someone, but often it is eventually unfair to everyone.

Take rent control. Rents are frequently one of the first things controlled in an inflationary period. After all, a lot of people pay rent, and there are more renters who vote than landlords. But if rents are frozen, costs are not. Thus, the landlord pays more for heat, light, taxes, and maintenance, until finally his costs closely approach his rental income. At that point he cuts down on maintenance and the building begins to deteriorate.

More important, there is so little return on the investment in the building that it loses value. After all, the value of any investment depends in great part on what it is able to earn. Furthermore, as the return dwindles on rental property, so does the construction of new rental property. Who will build when he knows that the return will be inadequate?

Thus, the supply of living space drops and the upward pressure on rents (demand-pull) intensifies. Eventually rents rise, and since costs do likewise, there is still no stimulation of supply, no new construction. So rent control does not keep rents down, long term; on the contrary, it pushes rents up by keeping the supply down in the face of rising demand.

Another example of this failure of controls to curb inflation was the recent attempt to control chemical fertilizer prices. Foreign demand was so strong that U.S.-produced fertilizer was shipped abroad, where it could get higher prices. Controls in this case meant a shortage of fertilizer at home.

PRICE STABILITY EQUALS UNEMPLOYMENT

The sad truth is that controls of wages and prices will not work. The only thing that will work to control inflation is a reduction on the demand side of the supply-demand equation. This means stiff taxes, reduced corporate earnings, and a relatively high level of unemployment.

Economists have estimated that we would need an average level of unemployment of nearly 8% to keep personal income down enough to hold prices stable. An unemployment rate of this magnitude on an average basis would mean an unemployment level in the nation's urban centers of something close to 30%. Obviously, this would produce considerable social unrest and perhaps political upheaval as well.

Most governments have decided that such a high level of unemployment is not worth the risk. They have opted for more inflation than they like instead of more riot and revolution than the system can stand. We believe that this decision has been a wise one and suspect future governments, even conservative ones, will take the same option—relatively low unemployment, say under 6%, and inflation of 5% or 6% a year—as a fair trade-off for social and political harmony.

Certainly the double-digit inflation of 1974 is intolerable to all, and has been cooled successfully. Nevertheless, inflation, easy to define and nearly impossible to control, seems a permanent fact of life. If so, we investors had better shape our investment plans accordingly, as we discussed in Chapter 10.

29

Money Supply

No discussion of investments, the stock market, or inflation can be complete without some comment on the money supply. Don't for a moment think the subject is too complex for you or that it is properly and primarily the preserve of bankers, economists, and governments. Baron Rothschild once quipped that only two persons in the world understood gold and the balance of payments, a director of the Bank of France and an obscure clerk in the Bank of England. Unfortunately, he added, they disagree. The same thing could be said about the money supply.

First, as a matter of definition, the money supply is simply the spendable amount of dollars around, be they cash in your pocket or a balance in your checking account. This is money, in short, that you can use if you have a mind to. Dollars in stocks or bonds, or in real estate, are not readily available and are not considered to be in the daily money supply.

The rise and fall in the supply of money depends primarily on the Federal Reserve Board. This venerable institution tries to keep the supply of money increasing fast enough to meet the demands of an expanding economy. Indeed, if the Fed did not increase the number of dollars available for us to work with, there would be no economic growth. It's not that an increased supply of dollars creates growth, but that a larger economy needs more dollars on which to function.

MONEY SUPPLY AND INTEREST RATES

A shortage of dollars means a sharp rise in interest rates and an inability to borrow money to build houses, finance inventories, or carry on business generally. The average auto dealer, for instance, borrows to carry his inventory of new cars. If money tightens and rates rise, he must pay more on his inventory loan until he reaches the point where his interest payments exceed his profit on sales. He is then out of business.

As far as interest rates are concerned, an *excess* of dollars, oddly enough, means much the same thing to the average businessman. Too many dollars means inflation of the demand-pull type—too many dollars chasing too few goods. Such inflation is promptly translated into interest rates which again, if they get high enough, can be a hardship to our auto dealer.

BALANCE IF YOU CAN

So, a reasonable equilibrium in the growth of the total supply of money is a must for an orderly economy. Achieving that balance is easier said than done. A reasonable equilibrium would mean a huge outpouring of dollars at Christmastime when everyone is buying presents for everyone else, or Christmas would be lean indeed; but in January, when we begin to recover from our holiday spending sprees, a reasonable equilibrium may mean virtually no growth in the money supply.

So it goes through the year—strong demand for dollars in some months and very little in others. If the Fed fails to meet the need for dollars when demand is strong it can put a real crimp in the economy. It can literally spoil a good rate of business growth with all the misfortune that implies—lost jobs, closed factories, business failures. If, on the other hand, the Fed does not recognize the periods of excess supply it will stimulate inflation and run the risk of creating a superheated economy—a boom that eventually must bust.

PITY THE FED

As if these hazards weren't enough for the hardy souls who run the Fed, consider the indirect and wobbly nature of the tools they have to work with. To increase the money supply the Fed buys government bonds on the open market. This gives the banking industry dollars which it can lend to you and me to run our lives and our businesses. Simple enough. But how many bonds need to be bought to release how many dollars?

To decrease the money supply, the Fed does the opposite. It sells bonds on the open market. By selling bonds it soaks up dollars that otherwise could be lent to such borrowers as thee and me. Here again, how much is enough? Many is the time that the Fed has moved cautiously into the bond market, selling bonds to absorb dollars and thereby cool an inflationary trend, only to learn later that instead of shrinking, the money supply had actually grown during that period.

This is not to cast doubt on the ability of our money managers at all, but merely to show how difficult it is for them to know, first, what the money supply is, second, whether if left alone it will expand or contract, and third, what effect their actions are likely to have.

WHICH WAY THE WIND?

The Fed has one more misery. That is to determine where the economy is headed and what should be done to the money supply to control the heading. The Fed tends, in this respect, to "lean into the wind." In other words, if the economy seems to be expanding strongly, the Fed tends to be conservative, to limit money supply growth. If things seem to be slowing down it eases up on the "money brakes."

The idea is to keep our economic growth on an even keel, to avoid boom and bust, on the one hand, and economic stagnation, on the other. Working as it does with imprecise visibility and inexact tools, the Fed is frequently wrong. For this it takes a lot of abuse, particularly from those who do not bear the heavy responsibility, who do not have to put their reputations where their words are.

The University of Chicago economist Milton Friedman gained his renown for "proving" that the Fed was always wrong, that when it leaned against the wind the breeze was always about to reverse. Professor Friedman believes that informed, educated, and experienced human judgment in this area is more often wrong than right. Thus he has persuasively urged the Fed for years to forgo any attempt to control the economy through expansion and contraction of the money supply. "Just increase it a fixed 3% each year to accommodate economic growth," says Professor Friedman, "and let the business cycle take care of itself."

IT AIN'T EASY

I mention Dr. Friedman's point of view only to illustrate how tough the Fed's job is. It does indeed face an important task which has the vaguest of parameters—and with tools of a very loose nature. So naturally, it is often wrong. But this is all the more reason for investors to keep an eye on the Fed's action, for when it moves in error it can really upset the applecart.

For instance, take early 1962 when the Fed tightened money to slow an incipient boom. It applied the brakes too hard on an economy that later turned out to have been slowing of its own accord. The result was a sudden shortage of money and a near credit crisis. The stock market promptly fell apart.

Admittedly the chart, which purportedly illustrates the charge that as the money supply goes, so goes the stock market, is difficult to read. That is because changes in the money supply are always small, albeit lethal. It doesn't take much cyanide to do

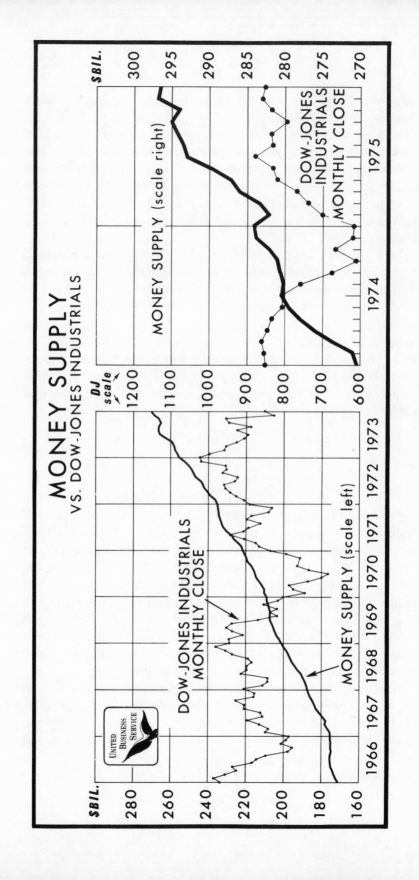

MONEY SUPPLY
VS. DOW-JONES INDUSTRIALS

someone in. But if you look closely at the chart you will see that the rate of growth did slow in 1969, 1971, and 1973, and in each case the stock market followed with a sizable decline.

So don't leave the money supply to the economists. Watch it yourself. When you see by the papers that the rate of growth of the money supply is slowing, get ready to batten your hatches—stormy stock market weather may be ahead.

30

Panics We Have Known

There is hardly a person in our country today who has not heard of the dreadful days of 1929 when stock prices crashed, major corporations plunged into bankruptcy, and millions of honest little citizens became destitute overnight.

So pervasive is the story of that fearsome week in October 1929 when the Dow Industrials fell 70 points in two days—a drop of more than a fourth—and the ensuing Great Depression when unemployment reached the epidemic proportions of 25% of the work force (we consider 6% intolerable today), that every Democratic presidential aspirant from Franklin Roosevelt to Adlai Stevenson campaigned against the hapless Herbert Hoover. People, being naturally fearful of what is only vaguely understood, still look for a repetition of that disaster whenever the stock market turns down.

Since the market always falls faster than it rises, stock market commentators have many opportunities to headline articles with such scary words as, "Biggest drop since 1929." Clearly, that year remains a major landmark in stock market, and national, history. We should review briefly here just what went on then, and why.

PEOPLE'S CAPITALISM

The great stock market boom of the 1920s represented, among other things, the first experiment with a "people's capitalism." In the past, investment in securities was largely reserved for the affluent and sophisticated. But in the 1920s the average man got a chance to get rich quick on Wall Street. He was aided by an environment largely free of regulation which left him and the brokers who served him bounded only by the limits of their avarice.

He was encouraged, for example, to buy stocks on a 10% margin with every penny he could raise. As the market rose, driven up by a host of fellow amateurs on similarly slim margins, he was encouraged to "pyramid" his holdings. This meant using securities bought on narrow margins as collateral for loans which were in turn invested in more stocks. By the end of the boom this left clerks and cabbies, harlots and housewives, even policemen and firemen, holding hundreds of thousands of dollars worth of common stock on the merest string of cash.

This "people's speculation" was compounded by the titans of industry and commerce who should have known better. As we pointed out earlier, investment trust managers were blatantly gambling with other people's money. The big industrial corporations were manipulating their own stock and risking their own working capital in the high-yielding commercial paper market. Meantime, while all of this fun was being had by people out after something for nothing, the business cycle was gradually slowing down.

THEN CAME THE DELUGE

In fact, the last few years of the booming 1920s were not really booming on the fundamental level of sales and earnings, employment and assets, or exports and imports. The boom was more and more in the minds of men. Caution was thrown to the winds as the assumption grew that the business cycle was over, that a new era of continuous growth was at hand, that what went up no longer must come down.

Just about this time the Fed, then not nearly as sophisticated as it is now, tightened credit. With everyone, individuals and institutions, loaned and borrowed to the hilt, the result was catastrophic. One called loan forced the call of another in a geometric progression, and the whole house of cards tumbled. The result was economic ruin for the nation and much of the rest of the Western world. It left a legacy of subsequent political upheavals, of which FDR's New Deal was by far the mildest.

CAN IT HAPPEN AGAIN?

So traumatic were the Crash and the Great Depression that investors to this day fear a repeat performance. Of course, the farther one's birthday is from October 1929, the less one tends to be apprehensive, but even later generations of investors harken to a prophecy of "another 1929."

So let's look at the differences between then and now. They are legion. Working first from peripheral environment to the core, let's consider the world we live in. In 1929 Europe was financially destitute and in social upheaval. Today Europe is economically stronger and politically more stable than ever before in history. Consider the Common Market and the upward revaluation of European currencies as examples. Japan, today's third greatest economic power, was little more than a feudal isle in 1929.

International cooperation then between us and "them" was nil. Today all trade and monetary matters are thoroughly discussed, negotiated, and compromised in order that they be the least unsettling to trade and monetary exchange as is humanly possible. Domestically, no one can borrow the way we used to. Today's homeowner begins to pay back his loan the day he takes out his mortgage. In 1929 there was no need to pay back capital. Monthly mortgage payments consisted only of interest.

DEBT NOW IS FINITE

Today one is discouraged from borrowing against security holdings to raise money to buy stocks. Margin requirements have been held right around 75% for the past decade or so (though they are now at a "low" 50%) versus the 10% level of 1929. Brokers' loans today run at only one third of the 1929 level in a vastly larger stock market. Thus, today's stock market decline cannot produce a wave of foreclosures. A decline in stock prices cannot feed on itself as it did four decades ago.

The Fed knows better now. Although it can, and does, still make mistakes, it would never again yank credit so tight in such an overborrowed market as it did then. Actually, it would never let the market get so overborrowed in the first place. We know a lot more about economics now. After all, that was before Keynes, and we are living with Galbraith, Samuelson, Friedman, and Eckstein.

Although it is sometimes hard to believe, investors today are more sophisticated and knowledgeable. Institutions, for instance, run presumably by well-educated professionals, account for about two thirds of the trading these days. Security trading, then almost without regulation, is now tightly regulated by the industry and briskly policed by the Securities and Exchange Commission. Last, common stocks today are vastly cheaper on better-accounted earnings than they were in the halcyon days of the flapper.

So, a major stock market break can happen now, but it is highly unlikely that it would match the 1929 debacle. Don't worry about it.

THE PANIC OF 1937

The next big bust in stock prices occurred in 1937 when it looked as though the recovery from the Great Depression was faltering. The market at that time was not undermined by excess debt, speculation, or tight credit, because people saw the slowing of business and feared a return to the depressed early 1930s. It was in 1937 that President Roosevelt coined the word "recession," meaning a mini-depression. His description was accurate, for that is all that occurred and, for that matter, all that we have experienced since. Depressions are, apparently, a thing of the past.

The Dow Industrials dropped almost 50% in a very short time in 1937. In so doing, they vastly overreacted to the mild business downturn that developed.

THE MISSING "BUSTS"

So it was with the big post–World War II drop in 1946. That year, the Dow tumbled from 212 to 160, a decline of roughly one fourth. This decline was brought on by fears of a classic postwar recession, which never really occurred. People were certain that just because World War I had been followed by a quick bust the much bigger and longer World War II likewise would be. It wasn't.

By 1950 the market had recovered and then was stimulated by the industrial boom generated by the war in Korea. This took the Dow Industrials to the dizzying heights around 290 when again recession fears brought a sharp drop to 254, a decline of only 12%. This was a good thing, for the slowdown in growth of the gross national product was slight. Three years later, stock prices tumbled again. This time the decline carried 20%, from 520 to 416, and the recession was a bit more pronounced. This was the downturn in which many voices clamored for federal action, lest we slip into a depression. But President Eisenhower stood firm in his opposition to vast increases in federal spending, and the economy recovered nicely, quite on its own.

GET AMERICA MOVING AGAIN

The latter years of the 1950s were relatively sluggish. The rate of inflation was pleasantly low, about 2% annually, and people felt pretty good. But GNP growth was modest and corporate profits actually declined in four years—1951, 1952, 1957, and 1958. It was a period of "profitless prosperity," some said. This may have helped put John Kennedy in the White House, for he promised to "get America moving again." He did, or someone did, because the stock market took off from 620 to 740 on the Dow in 1961, President Kennedy's first year in office.

The panic of 1962 was of political as well as economic origin. After soaring to an average price-earnings ratio of 22, stock prices dropped 25% that spring when Mr. Kennedy slapped down the steel industry for raising prices in defiance of his inflation-curbing guidelines. Brother Bobby, the attorney general, got the steel magnates out of bed in the dead of night for a White House head-cracking, and President Jack was widely quoted as saying, "Father always told me that businessmen were sons of bitches, and now I see why."

Wall Street immediately envisioned "socialism"—government ownership of the means of production—and fled from stocks. But it was not to be. U.S. Steel remained free. What's more, no recession developed. Both corporate earnings and GNP plodded steadily ahead for the next four years. This was yet another example of a panic on Wall Street that failed to represent the economy. In fact, this was one of those market declines that prompted Nobel Prize–winning economist Paul Samuelson to observe later on, "The stock market has forecast six of the last three recessions."

THE FIRST CREDIT CRUNCH

To prove that it could still err, the Fed pulled the credit drawstrings tight in the summer of 1966 and set the stock market on its ear. The Fed was simply trying to cool a boom that was beginning to show some signs of heating up. When the sledgehammer of tight credit landed on the tack of modest speculative excess, credit crumpled completely.

The stock market followed suit with a precipitous plunge of some 25%. Although corporate profits eased off in the next few years, GNP forged steadily ahead and stock prices slowly recovered. The 1966 panic cooled a lot of investors toward the market, and it was three years before prices returned to the prepanic high. During this period many investors turned to mutual funds as an alternative to their own obviously unsuccessful efforts.

THE MUTUAL FUND BUBBLE

The great boom in mutual funds that followed was one of the prime causes of the next panic, which was a big one. From a December 1968 high of just under 1000 on the Dow Industrial Average, stock prices plummeted 37% to a 1970 low of 630, the largest break in 33 years, since 1937.

The mutual funds did it almost single-handedly. In competing with one another for the investor's money, they invented the performance game (see Chapter 17). Fund vied with fund for ever better net asset value gains over shorter and shorter periods of time. Portfolio turnover soared, in some cases to 300% per year, and in many to 100%. More and more speculative and newly issued unseasoned shares were used. Assumed risks grew alarmingly.

When the bubble burst, losses were excruciating, so much so that many investors said, "Never again." They said it not only to mutual funds, whose assets shrank by the month as redemptions swamped new sales, but to common stocks generally. Even though corporate earnings moved up impressively in 1971 and to an all-time high in 1972, stock prices stumbled along slowly.

By early 1973 the Dow-Jones Industrial Average had barely returned to the 1000 mark. Even so, soaring corporate earnings had brought the price-earnings ratio of the Dow Industrials down to 14, well below the decade's average of 17. People just didn't trust stocks. The average P/E had been much higher at previous market tops. It had been 17 at the 1968 high, 18 at the 1966 high, and 22 in 1962.

WATERGATE, OIL, AND INFLATION

The most recent stock market panic, the 1973–74 tumble from 1050, had three components. Prices started down on news that price controls were all but being abandoned in the face of a concurrent announcement of the biggest jump in food prices in history. The Dow promptly tumbled 100 points from January to April as inflationary fears soared, taking interest rates with them. The banks' prime rate hit 10% for the first time ever.

Then in the spring and summer a series of political scandals in the Nixon Administration cost the government one vice president, three attorneys general, and nearly all of the senior White House staff. Prices fell another 100 points. In the fall, the Arab-Israeli war and the ensuing oil boycott and energy crisis took the Dow down the rest of the way.

Unlike other panics, this one came from sources really outside the business community. It was government action and inaction, scandal at home, and diplomatic disaster abroad that knocked the spots off the stock market rather than the sober fundamentals of earnings, assets, and dividends. Corporate profits soared in 1973–74, slipping only a modest 15% in 1975. Even this was in the early months, with strong recovery coming along later in the year. Total dividends kept right on rising.

WHAT ARE THE LESSONS?

What does it all prove? What has this series of panics demonstrated? A number of things. First, the market always goes to extremes. Don't trust it when everything looks great, and don't despair when all looks bad. Second, things that usually upset a bull market, that start the slide into bear markets, are largely unforecastable. You can tell when things are getting pretty euphoric in a general sort of way, but the chances of actually picking the top are poor. The market may quit early, as it did in 1973. Or it might go on a long binge of speculation as it did in 1964, 1965, and 1966. The most you can do is hold back on new buying when the market seems to be on the high side of its historical range.

The third lesson in all this is that market lows are as sudden and sharp as tops are usually broad. Pinpointing a low is impossible, then. Don't try. But just as you go easy on the buy side in lofty areas, postpone selling when the average price-earnings ratio is low.

And, of course, if you do have some money to invest, put it in the market when things are depressed. Sooner or later, you are bound to look like a winner.

Epilogue
A Simple Exchange
of Correspondence

THE BACK YARD

For those who sometimes wonder if these querulous and contentious times don't prove that the West is going to hell in a hack, a glimpse at this current comment by the London *Economist* should bring solace.

> ". . . the western system has shown that it is better at producing the material goods people want, even if it does also produce a lot of pollution in the process. It is better at adjusting itself to the wishes of the governed; an election is a cheaper and tidier way of arranging a change of government than burning down the party headquarters in Gdansk. And there is no comparison between the conformity which Russia demands of its friends in eastern Europe and the relatively loose relationship between the United States and its allies in western Europe."

To be sure, the myriad interests of the Free World are pulling and hauling at such a rate that one could wonder what hope there was. The truth seems to be that such apparent chaos is simply the human condition, that the confusion seems worse than it really is, and that despite it all we seem to get ahead eventually anyway.

At least that's the way it's been and we have every confidence 1972 will be just the same.

Happy New Year!

DECEMBER 27, 1971

Dear Mr. Sargent:

What I, as a feckless wretch of a would-be investor, would like in your book is not merely a litany of all the golden opportunities I booted. I want to know what I *should have been doing* to have educated myself. For example, going back to UBS in 1962, what were you recommending in growth stocks (Chapter 5)? Were you calling them right at the time? When I sat dumbfounded as C&O lost 26% in a morning, could I have gone back a few issues of UBS and seen that you were advising me to bail out? When I sold Sinclair in panic, then watched it go up another 55 points, were you telling me to hang on? What was the conventional wisdom about Equity Funding, Penn Central, IOS or whatever? It does me no good to have you tell me I could have picked the right ones *now*. You have to show me that there are fundamental *principles* at work, and if I had learned them in 1962, I'd be wealthy today.

For a specific, take page 231, and the discussion of AMF and the "bowling fad of the late 1950s." In your dusty archives there must be analyses of AMF: What were you recommending? What were others saying? On page 129 you say there'll always be a growth stock, but yesterday's growth is today's neoplasm, and how do you tell which is the malignancy? McGeorge Bundy tongue-lashes the colleges, and they all go out and squat and strain to achieve growth, and McGeorge Bundy is an honorable man.

Indeed, I am left with the peasant suspicion that the stock market is still an arcane institution. People don't invest in a company because they think it's good: they invest because they are betting that *others* will think it's good. In a horse race, you bet on a nag to win. In stocks, you bet that others will bet. Adam Smith's book *The Money Game* caught this flavor for me; he was the urbane cynic who didn't believe in the system, but who still played for the excitement. But your book is one written by a true believer for other true believers. I want to believe, Lord: help thou my unbelief.

F.W.

Dear Feckless:

You miss the point of my entire effort. Your paranoia shows. You insist that the world, or at least the investment community, is a vast conspiracy, of which you are the hapless centerpiece, the perpetual victim.

Not so. The financial community normally exists in a stew of simple confusion, laced at times with hysteria. There are, however, a few truths which, if religiously observed, will carry the true believer through any number of "bad times" to true riches.

These are:

1—The U.S. economy always has, and presumably always will, grow on average, if not every year and every quarter.

2—As the economy grows, as GNP swells, so must the average company as it meets the expanding demand of more people, rising living standards, new technology, etc.

3—As these companies participate in an expanding GNP, so must their average earning power.

4—And profit being the *sine qua non* of stock prices, higher per-share profits means eventually higher stock prices.

5—Waves of enthusiasm and depression will continue to sweep the financial community at erratic and unpredictable intervals, thereby elevating and depressing stock prices to temporarily unreasonable levels.

6—No one has ever been able to call these shifts of emotion with enough accuracy to stay even with the game, let alone to make real killings. On this point it is well to note that the killings made by the big traders of the early years on Wall Street were made by men who made the waves. It is illegal to make such waves now.

7—Worry not about tomorrow's price for Pullman or yesterday's price for Xerox. Just buy the stock of a strong company that seems a reasonable value today and sit with it until something seems to be changing in the company's basic situation—aging management, product obsolescence, vanishing market, new and vigorous competition—or the price of the stock has been whirled up to the stratosphere by some current hysteria. Then, in either case, sell and use the money to buy something that looks better.

Lastly, my dear Wretch, remember more investors have made more money on Wall Street with the seat of their pants than they ever have with their trading wit.

D.R.S.

Index

Index

About the Author

David R. Sargent has been applying his talent for transforming complex economic and investment matters into terms the layman can understand for nearly three decades. He joined United Business Service Company in 1946 following World War II military duty and became its president in 1961. He holds a degree from Dartmouth College and has done graduate study at Boston University, Northeastern University, and Harvard Business School. Mr. Sargent is a director of one of the largest savings institutions in New England and has been active in business and community affairs for many years.